The Axe is Laid unto the Root

by

R. L. Brandt

Segen Books
Black Forest Press
San Diego, California
May, 2003
First Edition

The Axe is Laid unto the Root

by

R. L. Brandt

**PUBLISHED IN THE UNITED STATES
OF AMERICA
BY
BLACK FOREST PRESS
P.O. BOX 6342
CHULA VISTA, CALIFORNIA
91909-6342
1-800-451-9404**

"And now also the axe is laid unto the root of the trees."
Matthew 3:10

***Unless otherwise noted, all scripture quotations are from the King James Version of the Holy Bible.

Cover Design: Aurora Zhivago

Disclaimer

This document is an original work of the author. It may include reference to information commonly known or freely available to the general public. Any resemblance to other published information is purely coincidental. The author has in no way attempted to use material not of his own origination. Black Forest Press disclaims any association with or responsibility for the ideas, opinions or facts as expressed by the author of this book.

**Printed in the United States of American
Library of Congress
Cataloging-in-Publication**

DEDICATION

To Marian, my wife of more than sixty years,who has been my coun-selor, my editor, and my computer operator in the production of this book, and who shares my passion for repentance in our individual lives, in our churches, and in our country.

FOREWORD

When true conversion takes place, the Holy Spirit launches the individual on a path leading to godly sorrow for, and abandonment of, one's sins. This process only takes place with the Holy Spirit's assistance.

Dr. Robert Brandt has written this excellent volume on repentance that will establish the work of God in the believer's life. The book's contents flow out of the author's many decades of study and successful ministry. Brandt is practical and balanced. What he has written in this book applies to every believer's life. Pastors, evangelists, missionaries, and all Christian workers will find these pages rich with excellent resources that are theologically sound and biblically based.

The author does not suffer the reader through "paralysis of analysis." As I read the book I was amazed that the Holy Scriptures contain so much on repentance.

Theologian Millard J. Erickson defines repentance as "godly sorrow for one's sin and a resolve to turn from it."[1] This definition is at once simple and profound.

Repentance involves action. A whole list of action words are involved in its definition: regret, deplore, lament, remorse, grief, contrite, relinquish, surrender, leave, quit, discard, withdraw, etc.

Repentance and faith really cannot be separated from one another. From our faith in Christ as Savior and Lord should come a conscious moral separation, a forsaking of sin, and a growth in personal fellowship with God.

Repentance is prominent in both the Old and New Testaments. Perhaps the most familiar Old Testament passage is *2 Chronicles 7:14,* *"If my people, which are called by my name, shall humble themselves and pray, and seek my face and turn from their wicked ways; then will I hear from heaven, and will forgive their sin, and will heal their land."* Many times in the Old Testament, God, through His servants and prophets, called Israel to repentance, to turn from their transgression, and in *Isaiah 59:20, "he will come to Zion as Redeemer"* [2]

The New Testament employs several terms for repentance. One is *"to have a feeling of care, concern or regret."* *(Matthew 21:29)* Another New Testament reference deals with remorse and regret (*Matthew 2:3*). True repentance is actualized in a change of behavior.

Judas displayed remorse, but not repentance. Another significant way the term is used in the New Testament is to think differently about something.

Jesus gave repentance a conspicuous place in His preaching and teaching (*Matthew 4:17*). Paul called *"all men everywhere to repent"* (*Acts 17:30*).

In a major U.S. City,. the Christian bookstores were requested to submit titles of books dealing with repentance, they had on their shelves. Unfortunately, not one Christian bookstore in that city carried one book dealing specifically with repentance. That vacuum can now be filled with this excellent volume.

Don Argue, Ed.D., President
Northwest College, Kirkland, Washington

Erickson, Millard J. *Concise Dictionary of Christian Theology.* Baker Book House: Grand Rapid, Michigan, 1986

2. Otto, Michel, *Theological Dictionary of the New Testament.* Erdmans: Grand Rapids, Michigan. As cited in Erickson, Millard J. Christian Theology, Baker Book House: Grand Rapids, Michigan, 1985

TABLE OF CONTENTS

Foreword vii

Chapter 1 The Present Truth 1
Chapter 2 Repentance: What Is It? 5

(REPENTANCE IN THE OLD TESTAMENT)

Chapter 3 When God Repents 13
Chapter 4 Repentance—God's Idea 21
Chapter 5 Agents of Repentance 27
Chapter 6 Repentance and Consequences 37
Chapter 7 Repentance—Plea of the Prophets (Part 1) . . . 45
Chapter 8 Repentance—Plea of the Prophets (Part 2). . . 55

(REPENTANCE IN THE NEW TESTAMENT)

Chapter   9 "The axe is laid unto the root" 63
Chapter 10 Repentance and Rebirth 73
Chapter 11 Repentance and Personal Pentecost 79
Chapter 12 Repentance and Spiritual Renewal 87
Chapter 13 Repentance—A Lifestyle 97
Chapter 14 Repentance—Its Limitations 103

(REPENTANCE   IN   THE   REVELATION)

Chapter 15 Repentance and First Love 109
Chapter 16 Repentance and Doctrinal Aberrations 119
Chapter 17 Repentance "Unto Life" 129
Chapter 18 Repentance—Thinking With God 141
Bibliography 149

CHAPTER ONE

THE PRESENT TRUTH

Is there a "present truth" for the Church and for the world today, and if so, what is it? I firmly believe there is and that is the reason for this book. The "present truth" for the hour is, *"Repent ye therefore, and be converted, that your sins may be blotted out, when the times of refreshing shall come from the presence of the Lord,"* or as the RSV translates it, *"that so may come times of refreshing from the face of the Lord"* Acts 3:19.

"Wherefore I will not be negligent to put you always in remembrance of these things, though ye know them, and be established in the present truth" 2 Peter 1:12.

"My wife, Marian, and I were en route home from our camp for Seniors at Glacier Bible Camp near Hungry Horse, Montana. As we drove along, Marian was reading to me (a practice not uncommon with us) from the prophet Isaiah. Finally she came to *Isaiah 57:1. "The righteous perisheth, and no man layeth it to heart, and merciful men are taken away, none considering that the righteous is taken away from the evil to come."*

Both of us had read that passage numerous times before, but it had borne no particular message or truth to either of us. Yet this day it was different. It literally captivated our attention, so that for many long miles we pondered its meaning and discussed it.

Arriving home, as I was unlocking the door, I heard the telephone ringing. Fumbling with the lock, I finally got in and rushed to answer . The caller was my brother, Jay, advising me that our brother, Derb, had just lost his life in a combine accident. He knew no particulars except that one of our nephews had intercepted a call on his CB asking for an emergency vehicle to be dispatched to the Brandt farm where our brother had supposedly been killed. We had no other information than that.

After hearing nothing further for an extended period, and out of anxious concern, I finally called my brother's farm, hoping to learn what had happened. My sister-in-law answered my call and reported that Derb had not been killed in an accident. Rather he was harvesting the final field of wheat of the finest crop he had ever raised. In fact, the grain was so heavy that periodically his machine would plug with the shear volume. She had seen him get off the machine to unplug it, but when he didn't emerge from beneath it, she became concerned. She drove the quarter of a mile from the house only to find him under the machine stark dead. He had died from a massive heart attack.

It was then that *Isaiah 57:1* came rushing back into my mind, *"The righteous perisheth and no man layeth it to heart, and merciful men are taken away, none considering that the righteous is taken away from the evil to come."* For me that was the "present truth".

Truth is always truth. It is as absolute as God Himself. It is infinitely unalterable and unchangeable, despite the present-day notion that there is no such thing as absolute truth.

Man's perception of truth may be changed from time to time. It can be affected by numerous factors and influences. Man's church or religious background, his traditional views handed down from one generation to another, his personal experiences, his biases and prejudices, his preconceived ideas, all of these and more bear upon his view of truth.

Truth can be illustrated with a perfectly straight line. Man's concept of truth can be demonstrated with a very uneven line. At points he may be right on, while at other points he is far removed.

For example, who would deny that Saul of Tarsus was positive he was on the side of absolute truth when he with all his might sought to exterminate the Church. Surely he had not a doubt in his mind until that moment when on his way to Damascus he came face to face with Jesus. At that moment, he discovered how far removed he had been from the truth.

Scripture teaches us that *"when he the Spirit of truth is come he will guide you into all truth"* *John 16:13*. The unmistakable inference is that none can claim he has all truth. Yet, all are instructed to *"Buy the truth, and sell it not"* *Proverbs 23:23*. Truth must be our constant pursuit and goal. The Word of God and the Spirit of God together are unparalleled guides to truth.

A question we need to confront is, What did Peter mean when he spoke of the "present truth?" Was he speaking of an aspect of truth pertinent to the time being, or was he rather seeking to underscore the truth which was at hand? The RSV translates this particular section, *"and are established in the truth which is with you"*, and the NEB translates it, *"and are well grounded in the truth that has already reached you."*

R. Finlayson, in *The Pulpit Commentary on 2 Peter* wrote, "There are certain fundamental facts which are essential to salvation, and essential to the understanding of the rest; certain great doors, so to speak, without passing through which it is not possible to thread the winding corridors within, and gaze upon the glory of the inner shrine. I understand it to be these whose constant remembrance is here enforced. Earnest research after truth is part of the honor due to the God of truth. It were an error to confine ourselves to one set of truths, and still to any one aspect of them; yet there are some which are the key-note to the others, and the main channels through which life flows to the believer, and we must be established in them, and we must endeavor to 'have these things always in remembrance.'"[1]

Again he wrote, "In one way there was not need for putting them in mind; for he bears testimony courteously to their knowing these things, i.e. having a firm standing, in the truth that was with them (not the present-day truth, as is suggested by the old translation) [1]."

Even so, from another point of view, there is truth which can rightly be labeled "the present truth", and which is especially pertinent to circumstances or situations immediately at hand. As has already been noted, truth is always and eternally truth. Yet there are specific times and periods in the lives and experiences of individuals, and in the ongoing of the Church when certain aspects or facets of truth are brought clearly and forthrightly into focus by the Holy Spirit, with the intent of gaining certain ends.

By way of example, the "present truth" may be related to a particular time when the Holy Spirit applies, through the processes of conviction, an aspect of the gospel to the heart of a sinner or unbeliever. Or there may be a specific time when a segment of truth is especially apropos in the light of some known or unknown prevailing circumstance or condition.

Then there are times when a "present truth" is a word for a certain group of people, as when it is directed to a specific body of believers. I recall, in my earliest days of ministry, attending what we called a fall convention for the ministers and laymen of the North Dakota Assemblies of God, in Bismarck. The first speaker addressed a particular subject. The second speaker, having not heard the first speaker, addressed the same subject. And before the convention ended all five of the speakers had spoken on the same subject, having not collaborated to do so. I can assure you that all of us who had been present left the convention with the sense that we had heard a "present truth", that is, a truth suited to a prevailing condition, as though it had been tailored for it.

In addition there are points in history when a "present truth" applies to the whole Church world. By the 1500s, the important truth of justification by faith had become obscured by the debris of religiosity. Then, in the providence of God, Martin Luther rediscovered or uncovered that glorious and important truth. And it became a "present truth", reaching to the ends of the earth.

The same was the case when in the 1700s the profound truths of sanctification and holiness had for long gone begging. Whereupon the brothers, Charles and John Wesley, became persuaded that those were truths which desperately needed to be applied to their time and generation and thus they became the "present truth" circling the globe. Obviously they were always truth, but they needed to be revived and resurfaced and reinforced.

By the late 1800s, another extremely important truth waited in the wings for rediscovery. It was truth relating to the baptism with the Holy Spirit, with the initial evidence of speaking with other tongues. The Church fathers had long ago decided that that experience belonged only to the beginning years of the Church, and that it was not relevant to the modern Church. But then, almost simultaneously around the world, that glorious truth reemerged and became the "present truth" for the latter days. Now everyone knows it has proliferated until virtually the whole Church has been the benefactor.

Is there a "present truth" for the Church and the world today, and if so, what is it? I firmly believe there is, and that is the reason for this book. The "present truth" for this hour is *"Repent ye therefore, and be converted, that your sins may be blotted out, when the times of refreshing shall come from the presence of the Lord"* or as the RSV states it, *"that so may come times of refreshing from the face of the Lord" Acts 3:19.*

CHAPTER TWO

REPENTANCE: WHAT IS IT?

> *Repentance cannot be true, except there be a true love of God, and an utter detestation of sin, and a heavy contrition that we have ever committed it, and a steadfast resolution never to fall any more into it, and then improved in actual sincere endeavor, what in us lies to abound in good works, and fulfill that duty which God requires of us."* [5]

Whereas God *"commandeth all men everywhere to repent"* Acts *17:30*, it is a must that all men everywhere understand what it is to repent. Until men really understand what repentance is, they will not likely do it.

So, what is repentance?

Webster says repentance is "the action or process of repenting, especially for misdeeds or moral shortcomings." And he further indicates that to repent means to be sorry; to turn from sin and to dedicate oneself to the amendment of one's life, to feel regret or contrition, to change one's mind.

I invite the reader to join me in a search for a Biblical perspective on the subject, for the better we understand the more able we will be to obey our Heavenly Father's command and to more fully enjoy the benefits. I personally have no desire to find an "easy out", or to in any way tamper with the divine intent. I earnestly desire that truth shall be my guiding star, for in the end unadulterated truth always prevails. I fear that the modern church does not understand "repentance" to signify that powerful change of mind, heart and life intended, but rather has a watered-down version suggesting an emotional, sentimental experience connoting some kind of remorse or regret.

Actually repentance is a very weighty and meaningful word, which when understood properly requires the probing of the deepest recesses of men's souls.

Geoffrey W. Bromily says, "The prophets do not invent a special word for true repentance but make do with the common word for return....This carries with it a sense of turning back, i.e., after relapse, but not exclusively so, for sometimes the idea is that of turning from. In general, what is meant is an about-face. The turning is mostly to God... and what is turned from is evil conduct, previous conduct, violence, idols or sin... The question of standing before God is the question that really matters. All other things, relations with others, ...and the state, depend on it. Implied here is a strongly personal view of sin whereby individual faults are seen to result from a wrong attitude to God, e.g. infidelity in Hosea, rebellion in Isaiah, forsaking God in Jeremiah... In line with the personal view of sin is a personal view of repentance as turning to God with all one's being. This turning, or returning, as the prophets often call it, has three facets. (1) It means obedience to the will of God, i.e., unconditional recognition of God in conduct corresponding to his will... (2) It means trust in God in rejection of all human help and all false gods. (3) It means turning aside from everything that is ungodly."[2]

In a recent address on repentance, Dr. Terry Law, commented that in the Old Testament it is an outward action which is the mirror or the expression of the inward change of mind.

All of that relates to Old Testament concepts of repentance. But what are we to understand from the New Testament use of the word?

The first in this setting to employ the word was John the Baptist. He obviously thought of repentance as the means whereby one readies himself for judgment, and for inner change demonstrated by outward evidence. To him it meant not depending upon human lineage or religious connection for readiness to appear before God, but upon right relationship to God for that end. How vital a truth that is!

Quick on the heels of John's message of repentance, came Jesus with a very similar message, "Repent: for the kingdom of heaven is at hand" Matthew 4:17. What then did repentance mean to Him? It meant "a final and unconditional decision, in a once-for-all turning to God in total obedience... Not merely evil, but anything that might be put before God must be renounced..."[3]

For Paul repentance meant "a radical break with the past... Psychologically it involves remorse...but more deeply it is God's saving work...with its implications of death and renewal."[4]

Strong in his exhaustive concordance of the Bible says repentance means "to think differently or afterwards, i.e. reconsider (mor. feel compunction)."

Important and meaningful as all of these definitions and insights are, it is likely our best understanding will derive from illustration and Biblical application. Therefore, in each of several cases, I will state a simple definition of repentance, and then I will seek to illustrate it.

<u>Repentance is turning away from a way of life which is displeasing to God, to a way of life which instead is pleasing to Him.</u> Again Terry Law notes that "repentance is an inner change of mind, resulting in an outward turning back, or turning around, to face in a completely new direction. It is not an emotion. It is a decision to change our mind."

Who could better illustrate this than the prodigal son? In rash self-centeredness he forsook his father's house, choosing in its place a lifestyle totally foreign to all that was good and right. He companied with vile and evil persons, wasting all the resources his generous father had provided for him; and spending his time dissipating his energy, and, as was to be expected, he finally came to a woeful end. His money was spent. His friends deserted him. Likely his health was failing. His future appeared anything but good. Bleak would have been a generous term for it.

It took all of that to bring him to his senses, but thankfully it did, for one bitter day he woke up to reality. Even then he could have plunged blindly on. He could have added insult to injury. He could have, in terms of modern society, followed a pathway to drugs and crime and suicide, but he didn't. He repented! He made a good decision. He forsook his destructive and debilitating lifestyle. He began seeing value in what he had so thoughtlessly forsaken. He 'bit the dust' and swallowed his selfish pride, turning completely around. He had been traveling full speed ahead, away from his father's house. Now he began doing the exact opposite. His sights were fixed on home. That was wholehearted and genuine repentance.

<u>Repentance is bending one's knees before the Creator, rather than stiffening his neck against Him.</u>

My father was born in Germany. At age 14, after his father had died prematurely, he migrated to the U.S. He lived with an uncle and later the other members of his family, including his mother, also came to this country. As he grew older, he and his two brothers were known as the "roughnecks on the hill." Later he married and moved to a farm in northern North Dakota.

Attending church was not on his agenda. Sunday was for greasing his Model T and for chores around the farmyard. He had his own religion which was a combination of some cultic ideas and his own thinking. He smoked a pipe until his teeth were worn down, played cards, danced the polka till the house shook. Yet he figured that if anyone was going to heaven he was.

Then one day a neighbor dropped in and invited him to hear a young evangelist who was conducting meetings in our nearby schoolhouse. With no sense whatever of spiritual need, but merely to accommodate his friend, he agreed to attend. Squeezing himself into an eighth grader's desk, he sat listening while the young preacher expounded on the salvation of children.

He found himself heartily disagreeing with the preacher. He decided that if the preacher repeated what he had already said more than once, he would get up and publicly argue with him. And anyone who knew my dad knew he could have done it. And sure enough, the young preacher began going over the same material again, whereupon my father took hold of the seat in front of him to arise and confront the preacher.

But he never did. Instead, the preacher noted he turned pale, but just sat there. What he didn't know was that the very moment dad was to rise up, a really remarkable thing had happened. He was literally caught out of himself and from the ceiling he found himself looking downward at himself. Instead of seeing the good and righteous man who he thought he was, he saw the community's worst sinner. It totally devastated him, and he sat there until the service ended. Then he quickly exited and headed home.

En route home he determined he would shake off the strange happening in no time. But despite his best effort he couldn't free himself. And later he testified that always a voice deep within kept whispering, *"If you will just bow your knee."* But he couldn't bring himself to do it. Proud human knees don't bend easily. So a whole week passed. Each evening he walked alone in his fields pondering the strange happening. But that voice within was unrelenting.

Finally two whole weeks had gone by; yet he hadn't shaken that strange experience. Then, in the middle of the third week, one evening, when he was more than a half mile from home, finally he surrendered. He bowed his knee over a large rock and in a moment of time was transformed, much as the Biblical Saul of Tarsus.

On his way home he prayed that his wife, my mother, would have a similar experience. Amazingly, when he got home and got into bed, mother arose and, for the first time in her married life, knelt beside the bed. She had no explanation for her extraordinary behavior, but dad always felt it was evidence that God hears the cry of a newborn babe.

Dad did not tell a soul about his revolutionizing experience, but within two days, neighbors living a quarter of a mile down the road began saying, *"Brandt has got religion!"* And indeed he had. From then on for more than fifty years, the Bible was his chief delight, and he lived to see his entire family come to Christ.

Repentance for him was bending his knees before his Creator, rather than stiffening his neck to Him. How different that was for him than for the Jewish crowd, which refused to bow it's knees at the preaching of Stephen and which heard him say, *"Ye stiffnecked and uncircumcised in heart and ears, ye do always resist the Holy Ghost: as your fathers did so do ye" Acts 7:51.*

<u>Repentance is sorrowing over sin, rather than piously continuing on in it.</u> I doubt that there is a better example of such action than King David. It seems that the whole world knows he sinned grievously, but it is doubtful if men in general know of or understand repentance as he practiced it.

For him it involved confession when he was confronted. *"And David said unto Nathan, I have sinned against the Lord..."2 Samuel 12:13.* Alluding to the bitter experience which visited him after his sin, he cried, *"For day and night thy hand was heavy upon me: my moisture is turned to the drought of summer. Selah. I acknowledged my sin unto thee, and mine iniquity have I not hid. I said, I will confess my transgressions unto the Lord" Psalm 32:4-5.*

It involved a flood of tears. His affidavit was, *"I am weary with my groaning; all the night make I my bed to swim; I water my couch with my tears. Mine eye is consumed because of grief."* Again he cried. *"My tears have been my meat day and night; while they continually say unto me, Where is thy God?" Psalm 42:3.* Listen to him one more time as he bares his heart, *"My wounds stink, and are corrupt because of my foolishness. I am troubled; I am bowed down greatly; I go mourning all the day long" Psalm38:5-6.*

Repentance for David was no light and insignificant matter. For him it included confession, and groanings, and grief, and tears, and mourning and more.

It should be added that true repentance involves being *"made sorry after a godly manner... For godly sorrow worketh repentance to salvation... but the sorrow of the world worketh death" 2 Corinthians 7:9-10.* Sorrow after a godly sort is the turning around process intended by the word repent, as Paul indicated in his further word to the Corinthians: *"...what carefulness it wrought in you, yea, what clearing of yourselves, yea what indignation, yea, what fear, yea what vehement desire, yea, what zeal, yea, what revenge!" 2 Corinthians 7:1.* Boni fide repentance launches the repenter into a fresh start, a whole new beginning.

<u>Repentance is responding to God's appeal through His prophet or His preacher, by a kind of action which clearly demonstrates that repentance.</u>

The people of ancient Nineveh are a case in point. Jonah, God's uncooperative prophet had been given specific instructions to *"Arise, go to Nineveh, that great city, and cry against it; for their wickedness is come up before me" Jonah 1:2.* Only after drastic measures did Jonah finally go, *"and he cried, and said, Yet forty days, and Nineveh shall be overthrown" Jonah 3:4.*

What followed the prophet's declaration is a profound repentance, seldom repeated in human history. Here is the record: *"So the people of Nineveh believed God, and proclaimed a fast, and put on sackcloth, from the greatest of them even to the least of them. For the word came unto the king of Nineveh, and he arose from his throne, and he laid his robe from him, and covered him with sackcloth, and sat in ashes. And he caused it to be proclaimed and published through Nineveh by the decree of the king and his nobles, saying, Let neither man nor beast, herd nor flock, taste anything: let them not feed, nor drink water: but let man and beast be covered with sackcloth, and cry mightily unto God: yea, let them turn every one from his evil ways, and from the violence that is in their hands" Jonah 3:5-8.*

That is the kind of repentance that gets God's attention and calls forth His compassion and tender mercy. *"And God saw their works, that they turned from their evil way; and God repented of the evil, that he had said he would do unto them; and he did it not" Jonah 3:10.*

Repentance is restitution. Wholehearted repentance does not end with confessions of infractions and disobedience toward God, nor is it complete with turning away from things and practices displeasing to God, nor with bending of knees before Him, nor with sorrow over having transgressed, nor yet with humility demonstrated by turning to God. It also calls for restitution wherever and whenever possible and it is not the kind of restitution imposed or required by others, but it is the kind which springs unsolicited from the truly repentant heart. *"And Zacchaeus stood, and said...if I have taken anything from any man by false accusation, I restore him fourfold" Luke 19:8.*

In his book, *Mercy and Judgment,* F. W. Farrar, quoting Archbishop Wake, says , "Repentance cannot be true, except there be a true love of God, and an utter detestation of sin, and a heavy contrition that we have ever committed it, and a steadfast resolution never to fall any more into it, and then improved in actual sincere endeavor, what in us lies, to abound in good works, and fulfill that duty which God requires of us." 5

CHAPTER THREE

WHEN GOD REPENTS

> Therefore we understand that repentance, as it relates to God, is quite different than repentance as it relates to man. God never repents for evil, for He is incapable of evil. *"In Him is no darkness at all" 1 John 1:5.* His repentance has to do essentially with His dealings with men who do sin. His own righteousness requires that all sin be avenged with death, but when the guilty sinner repents, then it can be said (that) God repents, for He turns away from imposing the death penalty.

The earliest reference to repentance in the entire Bible is in *Genesis 6:6, "And it repented the Lord that he had made man on the earth, and it grieved him at his heart."* On the surface it appears that the Bible contradicts itself, for in *Numbers 23:19* it declares, *"God is not a man, that he should lie; neither the son of man, that he should repent"* while in *Exodus 32:14* it is written, *"And the Lord repented of the evil which he thought to do unto his people".*

The fact is, there are two different Hebrew words translated "repent" in the Old Testament. Comprehending the meaning of each of those will assist our understanding.

First is the word *nacham*, which according to James Strong, means—to sigh, i.e. breathe strongly; by implication, to be sorry, i.e. (in a favorable sense) to pity, console or (reflex.) rue; or (unfavorably) to avenge (oneself): —comfort (self), ease [one's self], repent (-er, -ing, self).

Second is the word *shuwb*. Again according to Strong, the word has a vast multiplicity of possible meanings. Thus we understand that the particular meaning to be applied must be determined in light of the context wherein it is found.

Following is the complete definition as provided in Strong's concordance.

Shuwb, shoob, root; to turn back (hence, away) trans. or intrans., lit. or fig. (not necessarily with the idea of return to the starting point);

gen. to retreat; often adv. again:—(break, build, circumcise, dig, do anything, do evil, feed, lay down, lie down, lodge, make, rejoice, send, take, weep) x again, (cause to) answer (+again), x in any case (wise), x at all, averse, bring (again, back, home again), call (to mind), carry again (back), cease, x certainly, come again (back) x consider, + continually, convert, deliver (again), + deny, draw back, fetch home again, x fro, get (oneself) (back) again, x give (again), go again (back, home), (go) out, hinder, let, (see) more, x needs, be past, x pay, pervert, pull in again, put (again, up again), recall, recompense, recover, refresh , relieve, render (again), x repent, requite, rescue, restore, retrieve, (cause to, make to) return, reverse, reward, + say nay, send back, set again, slide back, still, x surely, take back (off), (cause to, make to) turn (again, self again, away, back, back again, backward, from, off), withdraw.

Before commenting on "repentance" as I intend to apply it in its Old Testament setting, consider the meaning of repentance as it is applied to God Himself.

In the first instance *"...it repented the Lord that he had made man on the earth..."* the inference is that He sighed deeply, it gave Him sorrow, and as the verse adds in an apparent effort at clarity, *"it grieved him at his heart."* In other words, man's actions caused Him to turn His head away in utter disappointment. That is how God repents.

Yet in *Numbers 23:19* it is written, *"God is not a man that he should lie; neither the son of man that he should repent."* And again in *1 Samuel 15:29, "And also the Strength of Israel will not lie nor repent: for he is not a man that he should repent."* Why, we may question, does scripture in one instance indicate that God does indeed repent and in another firmly declare that He does not?

James Morison offers us some brilliant insight, when commenting on the later passage. He says, "He who is Israel's Victory, or He in whom Israel has victory, will not repent. In verse. 11 God was said to repent, because there was what appeared to be a change in the divine counsels. 'God gave Israel a king in his anger, and took him away in his wrath' (Hosea XIII. 11). But such modes of speaking are in condescension to human weakness. Absolutely with God there is no change. He is the Eternal Present, with whom all things that were, and are, and shall be are one. But even looked at from below, as this finite creature man looks at his Maker's acts, there is no change in the Divine counsels, because, amidst all the vicissitudes of human events, God's will moves calmly forward without let or hindrance. No lower or secondary motives influence him, no rival power thwarts him. One instrument may be laid aside, and another chosen, because God ordains that the instruments by which he works shall be beings endowed with free will."[6]

Also, commenting on the same passage, Matthew Henry says, "Men change their minds, and therefore break their words; they lie, because they repent. But God does neither. He never changes his mind, and therefore never recalls His promise. Balaam had owned (v. 8) that he could not alter God's counsel, and thence he infers here that God himself would not alter it; such is the imperfection of man, and such is the perfection of God. It is impossible for God to lie, Hebrews.6:18. And, when in scripture he is said to repent, it is not meant of any change of his mind (for he is in one mind, and who can turn him?) but only of the change of his way. This is a great truth, that with God there is no variableness nor shadow of turning."[7]

Therefore we understand that repentance, as it relates to God, is quite different than repentance as it relates to man. God never repents for evil, for He is incapable of evil. *"In Him is no darkness at all" 1 John 1:5.* His repentance has to do essentially with His dealings with men who do sin. His own righteousness requires that all sin be avenged with death, but when the guilty sinner repents, then it can be said that God repents, for He turns away from imposing the death penalty.

In other instances where repentance is indicated on God's part, it is never in relation to actions, or choices, or works on His part, but only in relation to wrong actions, or choices, or works on man's part. For example, in *Genesis 6:6*, when it states that "*it repented the Lord that he had made man,*" the point is that he was grieved over what the man whom He had made had done. He was not grieved over, nor did He have sorrow for what He had done. He knew from the beginning that His purposes would come to fruition ultimately despite the course chosen by some of His creatures.

It is for this reason that now we turn to repentance as it relates to men in the Old Testament.

Interestingly, the first employment of the word as it related to God's people did not have to do with their sin, but rather with their reaction in the face of war. "*...for God said, Lest peradventure the people* **repent** *when they see war, and they return to Egypt*" *Exodus 13:17.* In this instance the meaning of the word repent , as determined by its usage, is simply turn about face. They were fleeing from Egypt, but would now, in the face of circumstances, turn 180 degrees and return to whence they had departed.

Even so, the more common usage of repent had to do essentially with the sinful and evil ways of God's people.

In the outset we will give attention to one who outwardly repented of his evil deeds, but who gave no acceptable evidence of having truly repented. He was King Saul.

The oft-repeated words of the prophet Samuel to Saul in *1Samuel 15:22-23* sort of set the stage for our discussion of repentance as purported by the king. *"And Samuel said, Hath the Lord as great delight in burnt-offerings and sacrifices, as in obeying the voice of the Lord? Behold, to obey is better than sacrifice, and to hearken than the fat of rams. For rebellion is as the sin of witchcraft, and stubbornness is as iniquity and idolatry."*

Saul had received a pointedly clear command from the Lord through the prophet, *"Now go and smite Amalek, and utterly destroy all that they have, and spare them not; but slay both man and woman, infant and suckling, ox and sheep, camel and ass"1 Samuel 15:3.* The record of Saul's incomplete obedience is *"But Saul and the people spared Agag, and the best of the sheep, and of the oxen, and of the fatlings, and the lambs, and all that was good, and would not utterly destroy them: but every thing that was vile and refuse, that they utterly destroyed" 1 Samuel 15:9.*

When Samuel learned of King Saul's deviation, it troubled him so deeply that *"he cried unto the Lord all night" (vs. 11)*, and in the same verse God Himself testified, *"It repenteth me that I have set up Saul to be king."*

Confronted with the evidence of his abject disobedience, instead of forthrightly repenting for his misdeeds, Saul sought to divert responsibility to the people. *"But the people took of the spoil, sheep and oxen, the chief of the things which should have been utterly destroyed, to sacrifice unto the Lord thy God in Gilgal" (vs. 21).*

It was then that Samuel zeroed in on his rebellion and drew from him his confession, and what appeared to be his repentance. But it was a repentance forced by circumstances, which in reality was no repentance at all. It was purely a diversionary device, a means for conserving his kingship and his role as leader for Israel. And God was not to be deceived by his outward pretense.

Indeed, Saul's feigned repentance is a profound revelation of the difference between what outwardly may appear to be repentance, and what is genuine repentance. The pressure brought to bear upon Saul by both the evident facts and the certainty of penalty produced his admission, *"I have sinned."* Yet his lack of a true spirit of repentance shows through in his effort at avoiding responsibility by his excuse, *"I feared the people."* His overriding concern was his escaping penalty, and regaining favor. And there is little to indicate even a hint of genuine repentance. Samuel's obvious non-reversal of penalty generated only a dread of outcome without any change of attitude toward his transgression.

How much this is like our times, when in the multitudes conviction of sin is unattended with a spirit of heartfelt repentance. And how unlike the agonizing awareness of sin that provokes true repentance. When that is the case, *"I have sinned"* is not an easy-out, but an agonizing attempt at reconciliation with a holy heavenly Father. Setting forth of excuses is farthest from one's thought, but open-hearted confession, *"against thee, and thee only, have I sinned and done this evil"* is the anguished cry. So filled with self-loathing, and so agonized with being alienated from God is such an one, that punishment and position are not his concerns. Instead his whole being is absorbed with intense desire verbalized in the cry, *"Create in me a clean heart, O God, and renew a right spirit within me" Psalm 51:10.*

"Whether Saul was self-persuaded that he had not committed any sin (v.13) is, as we shall see doubtful. The probability is that he was conscious of uneasiness, but had no true conception of the enormity of sin. His feeling was that he had no wish to disown the authority of God, that it was a mere matter of detail, that his general conduct was exemplary, and that he followed the inner light which seemed just then to indicate another way of ultimately and substantially carrying out the command.

"So do men tone down their sins and regard them as venial. The prophet's words reveal God's estimate of the sin of disobedience. It is the cardinal sin (vers. 22,23). It cuts at the root of all authority. It is the assertion of a power and a wisdom over against the power and wisdom of the Eternal. It makes man a worshipper of himself rather than of God. It ignores the solemn truth that we "cannot serve two masters." It does dishonor to him whose commandments are holy, just, and good. It sows in the moral sphere seeds of evil, which, taking root, must widen the separation of man from God. It claims for the desires and dim light of a sinful creature a higher value in the determination of actions than is to be

attached to the purposes of the All-Perfect. To render it heinous charac-
ter more clear, the prophet asserts that it renders useless and even wicked
the most solemn acts of worship (v. 22; of. Isa. 1:11-15).

"No profession of religion; no self-denial in surrender of choice
property; no conformity with venerable customs, or obedience in other
particulars, will for a moment be accepted in lieu of full and explicit obe-
dience to the clear commands which God lays on man both in relation to
himself and mankind."[8]

Thus it can be concluded that there is no substitute for that kind
of repentance which in the eyes of God surges forth from the contrite soul
and broken spirit of the man who has beholden his sin in the pristine light.
That only is acceptable repentance.

We might also consider Esau, who carelessly sold his birthright
to satisfy the temporary pangs of physical hunger. In his day a birthright
was of the greatest consequence. In some respects it might be compared
with the presidency of the United States. With it came almost incomparable privilege, highest honor, and sacred responsibility. Both the
birthright and the presidency could be forfeited by the irresponsible
actions of the possessor.

In recent time we have witnessed our United States president,
William Jefferson Clinton, in a sense despising his "birthright." Purely
out of passion for his own physical satisfaction, he has brought upon himself the awful consequence of impeachment by the U. S. House of
Representatives, and all but expulsion form the highest office in the land
by the U. S. Senate. His quite obviously phony repentance could not
remove the consequences of his despicable actions.

For Esau it was little different. *Hebrews 12:16-17* warns, *"Lest*
there be any fornicator, or profane person, as Esau, who for one morsel
of meat sold his birthright. For when he would have inherited the bless-
*ing, he was rejected: for he found **no place of repentance**, though he*
sought it carefully with tears.

We need to note that there is a finality to certain actions which
cannot be changed by repentance. While true repentance gets the ear of
God, it may not undo the outcome of unwise decisions by man. Esau had
sold his birthright, and regardless of how much repenting he might do,
there was no regaining it.

"The essential moral of his (Esau's) history is this: being the
first-born of Israel, and so primary inheritor of the promises made to

Abraham, he set no store by the privilege, and so lost it irretrievably. In early life he so lightly esteemed his birthright as the eldest born (carrying with it, as is supposed, in the patriarchal age, the priesthood of the family, and in his case, as might be presumed, the custody and transmission of the promises) that he parted with it for the gratification of a passing appetite. His word on that occasion expressed the limit of his aims and interests: 'Behold I am at the point to die: and what profit shall this birthright do to me?'

"*Later in life he nevertheless presented himself to claim the blessing of the firstborn from his dying father, but found that he had been forestalled.*

"*It does not appear that he had meanwhile changed his mode of life or made amends for his former carelessness; still he felt now that he had lost something worth having, and was grieved exceedingly. But not even his 'great and exceeding bitter cry' availed then to recover what was forfeited. And so neither he nor his seed had part or lot in the Abrahamic promises: the time of opportunity was gone forever.*"[9]

There is in all of this a highly valuable lesson for us. Value highly the spiritual birthright which is ours, and yield not to the temptation to "sell" it for present and temporary satisfaction or for a "mess of pottage." Yet in this dispensation of grace there is space for repentance, but there is also room for bitter loss irretrievable by the most sincere repentance.

CHAPTER FOUR

REPENTANCE—GOD'S IDEA

> *"Repentance, though necessary, is not meritorious but a condition for receiving the gracious gift of pardon which God gives of His own goodness."*
>
> A. W. Tozer

"But if from thence thou shalt seek the Lord thy God, thou shalt find him, if thou seek him with all thy heart and with all thy soul. When thou art in tribulation, and all these things are come upon thee, even in the latter days, if thou turn to the Lord thy God, and shalt be obedient unto his voice (For the Lord thy God is a merciful God;) he will not forsake thee, neither destroy thee, nor forget the covenant of thy fathers which he sware unto them. For ask now of the days that are past, which were before thee, since the day that God created man upon the earth, and ask from the one side of heaven unto the other, whether there hath been any such thing as this great thing is, or hath been heard like it? Did ever people hear the voice of God speaking out of the midst of the fire, as thou hast heard, and live? Or hath God assayed to go and take him a nation from the midst of another nation, by temptation, by signs, and by wonders, and by war, and by a mighty hand, and by a stretched out arm, and by great terrors, according to all that the Lord your God did for you in Egypt before your eyes? Unto thee it was shewed, that thou mightest know that the Lord he is God; there is none else beside him. Out of heaven he made thee to hear his voice, that he might instruct thee: and upon earth he shewed thee his great fire; and thou heardest his words out of the midst of the fire." Deuteronomy 4:29-36.

Israel was little different than modern man. Their history is shot through with accounts of God's blessing, of their enjoying great victories and abounding prosperity, of their vacillating and turning away from God, of ultimate making idols of wood and stone, and bowing down to them, and their eventual experiencing the judgment of God.

In Deuteronomy Moses affords us a glimpse into the heart and mind of God. Repentance is no cleverly devised psychological scheme of man for expelling guilt resulting from his aberrant behavior. But it is a means borne in the compassionate heart of God whereby sinful man can be set on a course toward reconciliation with his heavenly Father. Yes, repentance is God's idea.

Repentance, as far as God is concerned, is a "second best". God's preference is that men need no repentance. For that reason he gave commandment to Adam. For the same reason He gave the ten commandments to Israel. And again, for the same reason Jesus, several times, instructed, *"And thou shalt love the Lord thy God with all thy heart, and with all thy soul, and with all thy mind, and with all thy strength: this is the first commandment: and the second is like, namely this, Thou shalt love thy neighbor as thyself. There is none other commandment greater than these." Mark 12:30-31.*

In no way was God seeking to exercise tyrannical ownership and control over His people. Their own best interest was His motivation. What He required of them was to their highest advantage, for He foresaw that to engage in anything which He had forbidden would certainly lead to their loss, and could ultimately lead also to their eternal destruction.

The notion that God is a cruel, domineering, demanding, severe, inconsiderate taskmaster misses the truth inestimably. The exact opposite is true. *"And the Lord God of their fathers sent to them by his messengers, rising up betimes, and sending; **because** he had compassion on his people"* 2 Chronicles 36:15. *"Like as a father pitieth his children, so the Lord pitieth them that fear him"* Psalm 103:13. *"But thou, O Lord God, art a God full of compassion, and gracious, longsuffering and plenteous in mercy and truth." Psalm 86:15.*

Scripture is replete with references to God's unmatched compassion, His overwhelming tenderness, His unparalleled long-suffering, His generous mercy and His abounding grace. And to see Him for who He truly is, is to begin grasping the monumental significance of the repentance He craves from His people, and from mankind everywhere. On the other hand, to experience genuine repentance is to see God as the great God who He is.

A young man of my acquaintance was in Bible College. While there he struggled with what he perceived to be a pressing need in his life. While he didn't fully grasp how great his need was, he did pray with earnestness about it. Then one day, no doubt in God's providence, one of the college administrators, who was also a teacher, addressed the students in a fashion that really captured his attention. The fact was, he spoke so directly to this student's pressing need that it made him all the more aware of his condition, resulting in his near panic.

It generated a crisis of no small consequence for him, resulting in a feeling of being utterly forsaken by God. His otherwise high aspirations for becoming a minister of the gospel seemed to lay in ashes at his feet.

What should he do? He hadn't a clue. He was too "out of it" to pray. To whom could he turn for help?

Sensing no direction and being completely overwhelmed by foreboding darkness, he retired to his room in the men's dorm. Knowing not what to do, he simply dropped to his knees at a chair, only immediately to sense God speaking to him and urging him to "open the Book".

Ordinarily I wouldn't advise anyone to just "open the Book" and randomly read what his eyes might fall upon for gaining guidance. That could be disastrous. In my judgment it is generally not a safe course to follow in pursuing knowledge of the Divine will.

(I recall a godly woman telling of seeing fierce-looking clouds gathering on the western horizon. Fear struck her heart, as she saw what could easily be a very destructive storm approaching. She rushed into her home, opened her Bible and began reading. Her eyes fell upon these words, *"And Jesus said unto them, See ye not all these things? ...verily, I say unto you, There shall not be left here one stone upon another, that shall not be thrown down" Matthew 24:2:1.* I assure you, she derived little comfort from that!)

But his case was different. He was young and inexperienced. He had never before faced such a crisis. He didn't know the Lord's way very well. He had a desperate need and he knew not where or to whom to turn. His only hope was in turning to God.

Obeying the impulse to "open the Book", he began to read: *"Sing, O heavens; and be joyful, O earth; and break forth into singing, O mountains: for the Lord hath comforted his people, and will have mercy upon his afflicted. But Zion said, The Lord hath forsaken me, and my Lord hath forgotten me. Can a woman forget her sucking child, that she should not have compassion on the son of her womb? yea, they may forget, yet will I not forget thee. Behold, I have graven thee upon the palms of my hands; thy walls are continually before me" Isaiah 49:13-16.*

He could not have discovered a passage in all of the Bible that so profoundly spoke to his dilemma.

His first reaction was, What do I have to sing about? What comfort and what mercy is available to me? In all his young life he had never been so uncomfortable or so distressed. He had always been a sort of free spirit full of song and life-joy. But now it was different. All of that was gone. His song had vanished, and he found himself identifying with verse 14, *"The Lord hath forsaken me, and my Lord hath forgotten me."* No words could have better described how he felt. But verses 15-16 brought new hope and light for his darkness. *"Can a woman forget her sucking child...? Behold, I have graven thee upon the palms of my hands."*

All that God desired and required from him was his turning (that was an attitude of repentance) to Him with his whole heart. To bring that about, He had employed the means He deemed necessary. He rose from his knees, his heart's cry answered and he went on to bless his fellow men.

God had the best of intentions for His people, Israel. He longed to share His great self with them. He intended to make Himself known to them. He planned that they should be the most blessed people on the earth. He desired that wickedness would be far removed from them. He certainly had no sadistic desire to see them degenerate to the point where repentance was necessary. Even so, if circumstances would arise to require repentance, He would want nothing more than to see them turn (repent) toward Him.

That is what Moses envisioned in Deuteronomy 4. On the one hand he envisioned Israel, blessed of God. His word is *"For what nation is there so great who hath God so nigh unto them, as the Lord our God is in all things that we call upon him for? And what nation is there so great, that hath statutes and judgments so righteous as all this law, which I set before you this day? Deuteronomy 4:7-8.*

On the other hand, he was keenly aware of the possibility of the same people turning away from their glorious privilege and heritage. More than once he cries, *"Take heed."* In verse 4 His cry is, *"Take ye therefore good heed unto yourselves."* And again in verse 23 He appeals, *"Take heed unto yourselves."*

And then he adds his passion-filled warning, *"I call heaven and earth to witness against you this day, that ye shall soon utterly perish from off the land whereunto ye go over Jordan to possess it; ye shall not prolong your days upon it, but shall utterly be destroyed. And the Lord shall scatter you among the nations, and ye shall be left few in number among the heathen, whither the Lord shall lead you"* Deuteronomy *4:29-30.*

Nevertheless, credit Moses with insightfuly discerning God's heart, for he perceived that even though Israel might foolishly depart from Him if under God-initiated tribulation she would turn again, that is, if she would sincerely repent, He would again demonstrate His tender mercy. *"But if from thence thou shalt seek the Lord thy God, thou shalt find him, if thou seek him with all thy heart and with all thy soul...even in the latter days, if thou turn to the Lord thy God...he will not forsake thee, neither destroy thee"* vs. *29-31.*

God has not changed, nor will he ever change. Before man ever was, He devised repentance as the doorway into His incomprehensible mercy and grace. Repentance, by itself could not result in God's approbation and forgiveness, for that would infringe upon His justice and His righteousness. Before sin and evil could be forgiven there must of necessity be the forfeiture of life, either the life of the transgressor or that of another who would choose to bear the guilt for him.

Thus the scriptures speak of *"repentance toward God, and faith toward our Lord Jesus Christ"* Acts *20:21.* It is God who is offended by sin, but it is also God who before the foundation of the world devised a plan whereby He could forgive the sin and yet remain the God of truth and justice that He is.

Repentance cannot and does not provide God's forgiveness. If it could, the forgiveness of God would be dependent on the works of man. Nay, rather, repentance *"toward God"* is but the key for opening the doorway to divine grace, and to *"faith toward our Lord Jesus Christ,"* who through His sacrificial death for sin, made it possible for God to be *"just and the justifier of him which believeth in Jesus"* Romans *3:26.* Thus the gift of forgiveness and salvation is free, the product of pure grace; but repentance is man's freewill act which invites it into his life. Repentance prepares the ground for the application of grace.

How vital it is, therefore, that mortal and sinful men, at least to a degree, perceive the heart and thought of God. While the scriptures indicate that man's thoughts and God's are not to be compared, yet God has devised a means whereby man can, at least in a measure, discern the thoughts of God.

"For what person knows a man's thoughts except the spirit of the man which is in him? So also no one comprehends the thoughts of God except the Spirit of God. Now we have received not the spirit of the world, but the Spirit which is from God, that we might understand the gifts bestowed on us by God" 1 Corinthians 2:11-12 (RSV).

Satan could not be more pleased than when man is bereft of God's thoughts and unaware of God's benevolence and provision. To this end he exercises himself greatly. For the Bible reveals that *"the god of this world* (Satan) *hath blinded the minds of them which believe not, lest the light...should shine unto them"* 2 Corinthians 4:4. Also in *Acts 28:27,* Paul wrote, *"For the heart of this people is waxed gross, and their ears are dull of hearing, and their eyes have they closed; lest they should see with their eyes, and hear with their ears, and understand with their heart, and should be converted, and I should heal them."*

We need to understand that Satan is at work, employing every conceivable means for keeping sinful man unaware of the bountiful provisions God has made for enabling him to escape the awful consequences of his transgressions. For if and when he is unaware, and the *"sorrow of the world overtakes him, it worketh death"* 2 Corinthians 7:10. He is without God and thus without hope, and in not a few instances his fate is suicide.

What a vast difference there is when he is knowledgeable of God's desires and purposes for him, and also aware of the God-provided means (that is, repentance toward God, and in our time, faith toward our Lord Jesus Christ) for a whole new beginning.

God offered repentance to Israel. He now offers it to us.

CHAPTER FIVE

AGENTS OF REPENTANCE

> *Surely the agents of repentance come under the Divine indictment if all they do is bring people to the point of repentance. That would be like rescuing a drowning man from a raging river, only to abandon him to die of cold and hunger on the shore.*

"Say unto them, As I live, saith the Lord God, I have no pleasure in the death of the wicked; but that the wicked turn from his way and live: turn ye, turn ye from your evil ways; for why will ye die, O house of Israel?" Ezekiel 33:11.

Nowhere in the entire Old Testament is the compassionate heart of God more plainly in view than in the passage above. The death of the wicked pains Him beyond our comprehension, for who but He understands sins consequences and hells horrors? On the other hand, His delight in those who have repented is evidenced in David's cry, *"Precious in the sight of the Lord is the death of his saints" Psalm 116:15.*

Little wonder then that God has so profusely underscored the importance of repentance in the vast majority of Old Testament books. It is the single act which can spell the difference between eternal life and eternal damnation, for it is the first step toward reconciliation between sinful man and His holy God. Therefore in this chapter we will give attention to the Old Testament as it addresses the issues of (1) the need for repentance, along with agents of repentance, and (2) the results of repentance.

An agent of repentance is one who carries the good news of the availability of repentance to sinful men. He is one who uncovers and underscores man's need for repentance. He may project the profound fruits of repentance, and he may also underscore the folly of non-repentance.

A case can be made to show that God Himself was the first agent of repentance. While the ordinary elements of Adam and Eve's repentance may not be projected in scripture, the fruits are visible. *"Unto Adam also and to his wife did the Lord God make coats of skins and clothed them" Genesis 3:21.*

Interestingly, the second obvious agent of repentance was the Holy Spirit. *"And the Lord said, My spirit shall not always strive with man..." Genesis 6:3.* That declaration was provoked by God's evaluation of the deplorable conditions preceding the flood. *"And God saw that the wickedness of man was great in the earth, and that every imagination of the thoughts of his heart was only evil continually" Genesis 6:5.*

It appears evident that despite the perpetual and persistent strivings of the Spirit of God, intended to bring antediluvian man to repentance, it was to no avail. Here we must remind ourselves that God always honors free moral agency. He always has and He always will. He forces none to repent. Yet He offers and urges all to repent.

Prominent among men as agents of repentance is God's servant Moses. In the previous chapter, we viewed his concerted effort at bringing Israel to repentance. However, before his remarkable encounter with God on Mount Sinai, it appears that he saw little prospect for his sin-laden people, for we hear him pleading, *"Yet now, if thou wilt forgive their sin—; and if not, blot me, I pray thee, out of the book which thou hast written" Exodus 32:32.*

Nevertheless, after the eyes of his understanding were enlightened on Sinai, his perspective was effectively and forever changed. Rather than seeing God only as a God of severity and judgment, now he saw Him, first of all, as *"The Lord, The Lord God, merciful and gracious, longsuffering, and abundant in goodness and truth, Keeping mercy for thousands, forgiving iniquity and transgression and sin."* True, he also saw Him as the God who *"will by no means clear the guilty ..." Exodus 34:6-7.*

What he must not have understood until then was the God-ordained role of repentance, without which God could not simply and arbitrarily clear the guilty. Having seen that, he was thereafter to be seen vigorously encouraging and seeking to incite Israel to repentance.

Most prominent among Old Testament agents of repentance, beyond Moses, were Samuel, Solomon, David, Isaiah, Jeremiah, Ezekiel, Daniel, Hosea, Joel, Jonah and Zechariah. This is not to say that others were not agents. They most certainly were. But those named seem to stand out among all others. And let it be noted here that God highly val-ues everyone so engaged. The prophet Daniel stated it insightfully when he said, *"And they that be wise shall shine as the brightness of the firma-ment; and they that turn many to righteousness* (that is: bring many via repentance) *as the stars for ever and ever" Daniel 12:3.*

Consider Samuel, one of the outstanding Old Testament prophets. He was also a first-rate agent of repentance.

While he was Judge in Israel, Israel had demanded and obtained a king so they could be like the nations around them, much to the godly Samuel's consternation and displeasure. Israel's spiritual welfare was his chief interest and concern, but Samuel felt that when Israel, in spite of his passionate pleading, insisted on having a king, they were actually reject-ing him.

We should note here that agents of repentance, whether then or now, do have their disappointments. Not all men are disposed to repent, the most godly and concerted efforts of the agent notwithstanding. But God had a word of encouragement for the disconcerted Samuel. *"...they have not rejected thee, but they have rejected me, that I should reign over them" 1 Samuel 8:7.*

Yet despite his disappointment with the people and his conse-quent bout with discouragement, his compassionate concern for Israel did not wane. Anything he could do to spare Israel the judgment of God, that he would do, and that he did. Hear his urgent solicitation of Israel's atten-tion and their response:

"Now therefore behold the king whom ye have chosen, and whom ye have desired! and, behold, the Lord hath set a king over you. If ye will fear the Lord, and serve him, and obey his voice, and not rebel against the commandment of the Lord, then shall both ye and also the king that reigneth over you continue following the Lord your God: But if ye will not obey the voice of the Lord, but rebel against the commandment of the Lord, then shall the hand of the Lord be against you, as it was against your fathers. Now therefore stand and see this great thing, which the Lord will do before your eyes. Is it not wheat harvest to day? I will call unto the Lord, and he shall send thunder and rain; that ye may perceive and see that your wickedness is great, which ye have done in the sight of the Lord, in asking you a king. So Samuel called unto the Lord; and the Lord sent thunder and rain that day: and all the people greatly feared the Lord and Samuel. and all the people said unto Samuel, Pray for thy ser-

vants unto the Lord thy God, that we die not: for we have added unto all our sins this evil, to ask us a king" 1 Samuel 12:13-19.

It can be fairly stated that Samuel preached powerfully and persuasively. He withheld no punches and God confirmed his preaching with signs and wonders. And to his pleasure, the people did repent. However repentance is deemed genuine only if it is followed with evident fruit to validate it. While repentance is an act, it is also a lifestyle. Therefore, when repentance is only a single act, we have right to question its genuineness.

If repentance is merely an act precipitated by fear of consequences, or by a desire to appear righteous in men's eyes, or in an effort to hide from reality, it is doubtful if it is repentance at all.

Samuel's response to Israel's repentance was to give them positive guidelines on how they were to demonstrate their turning from their evil ways and unto the living God.

"And Samuel said unto the people, fear not: ye have done all this wickedness: yet turn not aside from following the Lord, but serve the Lord with all your heart; and turn ye not aside: for then should ye go after vain things, which cannot profit nor deliver; for they are vain. For the Lord will not forsake his people for his great name's sake: because it hath pleased the Lord to make you his people" 1 Samuel 12:20-22.

Nor was he unmindful of his own enabling role. *"Moreover as for me, God forbid that I should sin against the Lord in ceasing to pray for you: but I will teach you the good and the right way" 1 Samuel 12:23.*

It is not enough for the agent of repentance to merely bring people to repentance, essential as that is. But beyond repentance there is desperate need for guidance, lest the repentance fail in its purpose, and the repenter be swept back into his old ways as a result of his own ignorance or human weakness. In this instance, Samuel did two important things which become the agent of repentance. First, he recognized the importance of prayer for the repentant. In his eyes, he himself would be sinning should he fail to pray for them.

The Apostle Paul had a similar heart when he prayed for the newly converted Galatians. *"My little children, of whom I travail in birth again until Christ be formed in you" Galatians 4:19.* We may rightly wonder how many who are brought to true repentance fail because the agents of repentance stop short of their own duty and responsibility. Samuel would not be one of them.

Second, Samuel recognized he needed to do more than to pray. He must give "feet" to his prayer and become God's means to the answer by teaching Israel "the good and the right way."

Surely the agents of repentance come under the Divine indictment if all they do is bring people to the point of repentance. That would be like rescuing a drowning man from a raging river, only to abandon him to die of cold and hunger on the shore.

Solomon, too, was a God-ordained agent of repentance. For him God spelled out in readily understood terms his mission to Israel, but He also warned him of the dire results should he fail in his own assignment. Not only would he suffer the fearful consequences, but the hosts of those over whom he was king would also reap the sorry results.

Let us not forget that in this latter day, should we who are agents of repentance fail in our mission and divine assignment, by our own sinning, that others, and in some cases, many others, will experience the fearful fall-out. Here is the record of the charge which God gave to His agent of repentance.

"And if thou wilt walk before me as David thy father walked, in integrity of heart, and in uprightness, to do according to all that I have commanded thee, and wilt keep my statutes and my judgments: Then I will establish the throne of thy kingdom upon Israel for ever as I promised to David thy father saying, There shall not fail thee a man upon the throne of Israel. But if ye shall at all turn from following me, ye or your children, and will not keep my commandments and my statutes which I have set before you, but go and serve other gods, and worship them: Then will I cut off Israel out of the land which I have given them; and this house, which I have hallowed for my name, will I cast out of my sight; and Israel shall be a proverb and a byword among all people: and at this house, which is high, every one that passeth by it shall be astonished, and shall hiss; and they shall say, Why hath the Lord done this unto this land, and to this house? And they shall answer, Because they forsook the Lord their God, who brought forth their fathers out of the land of Egypt, and have taken hold upon other gods, and have worshipped them, and served them: therefore hath the Lord brought upon them all this evil"
1 Kings 9:4-9.

In 2 Chronicles 6, Solomon provides for us an insight into the heart of a true agent of repentance. He in no way wants repentance to be necessary; yet recognizing the likely failure of his people, he seeks to set the stage for such an eventuality. He does not easily turn them over for judgment.

We would do well to follow his example, for it seems that too often we tend to consign failing believers to judgment, rather than to applying ourselves to diligent efforts toward leading them to true repentance. There can be no doubt that such is the God-ordained way, for *Romans 2:4* challenges, *"Or despisest thou the riches of his goodness and forbearance and longsuffering; not knowing that the goodness of God leadeth...to repentance?"* Repentance must always and forever be our objective. Never judgment and damnation.

Listen to Solomon's heart for Israel: *"And if thy people Israel be put to the worse before the enemy, because they have sinned against thee; and shall return and confess thy name, and pray and make supplication before thee in this house; Then hear thou from the heavens, and forgive the sin of thy people Israel, and bring them again unto the land which thou gavest to them and to their fathers. When the heaven is shut up, and there is no rain, because they have sinned against thee; yet if they pray toward this place, and confess thy name, and turn from their sin, when thou dost afflict them; Then hear thou from heaven, and forgive the sin of thy servants, and of thy people Israel, when thou hast taught them the good way, wherein they should walk; and send rain upon thy land, which thou has given unto thy people for an inheritance."* 2 Chronicles 6:24-27.

And also note God's response, which might well be called the golden text for restoration, renewal, and revival.

"If I shut up heaven that there be no rain, or if I command the locusts to devour the land, or if I send pestilence among my people; If my people, which are called by my name, shall humble themselves, and pray, and seek my face, and turn from their wicked ways; then will I hear from heaven, and will forgive their sin, and will heal their land."
2 Chronicles 7:13-14.

Before turning our attention to the repentance aspect of this text, let us focus upon what may be termed the "Ifs" and "Thens" of God. Scripture is peppered with them.

Some hold the view that regardless of what men may or may not do, God is nonetheless disposed to do His own thing. It is contended that God is the Sovereign of the universe, and that ultimately man, at best, plays a very insignificant role in the final analysis. They are quite persuaded that God has predetermined the final state of all men and that therefore there is little, if anything, man can do about it.

However, it appears to me that in such a view, a major factor is overlooked, or possibly (God forbid) deliberately set aside. That is the Biblically announced and attested foreknowledge of God. *"I am God, and there is none like me, declaring the end from the beginning, and from ancient times the things that are not yet done..." Isaiah 46:9-10.*

For me personally, when I became aware of that profound foreknowledge, my theretofore concerns over predestination began dissolving, for it made room for man's free will while in no way denying God's sovereignty.

Indeed, man, the sovereign God's own creation, is, at His behest and in His own incomprehensible wisdom, a free moral agent. Otherwise we wonder how he could conceivably bring pleasure to the God in whose image he is. Were he a mere puppet, maneuvered at the will of another, it is extremely difficult to see how God could derive pleasure from him. It further appears highly perplexing, and quite irrational that scripture should place so much emphasis on man's choices. If those choices do not really matter, why then allow for them at all? Why the repeatedly declared "ifs" and "thens"? And why the "if" and "then" in the passage under consideration?

Yes, indeed, man has a most significant role. His own repentance for his own willful and sinful acts permits the sovereign God to do what He desires and intends for any and all of His Creatures.

In the passage under consideration, God's "ifs" require no great theological analysis. None need doubt the intent. Anyone can comply if he will. I think we tend to clutter and complicate God's declared requirements. For example, in our modern setting there is not an insignificant notion circulated that if folks will simply make a pilgrimage to some place, be it Toronto, Canada, or Pensacola, Florida, or Grand Rapids, Michigan, or Springfield, Missouri, or anyone of a number of other places, then they will experience restoration, renewal and revival for themselves.

While I think that such pilgrimages may have advantage in that being on the scene of a spiritual revival can stimulate faith and encourage personal involvement, I am also constrained to remind us that our God is wherever people choose to meet with Him. A mere two or three, gathered in a simple place in His name, invites His special presence. And after all, not many can make pilgrimages to distant places. Yet everyone can comply with God's "ifs" and subsequently experience His "thens".

Hence, I direct our attention to the "If" in verse 14. *"If my people, which are called by my name shall humble themselves, and pray, and seek my face, and turn from their wicked ways.."* Only a bit of attention will enable us to see that essentially two requirements are made whereby God's people can gain His promised "then".

The first is prayer. Prayer involves humbling one's self and seeking God's face. We need not complicate it, nor do we ever dare depreciate its importance or its certain necessity. Even so, prayer is but half of the divinely prescribed equation. It is at this point that I fear we fail at gaining the desired end, and at experiencing God's promised and gracious "then".

Admittedly, I possess little knowledge of chemistry. Yet I am aware of the formula for water: H^2O. It represents two parts of hydrogen to one part of oxygen. Both parts, as indicated by the formula and melded together, constitute water. Should it be possible for someone to possess all the hydrogen in the world, he would yet have no water. Again, should he possess all the oxygen in the world, he likewise would have no water. Only the proper combination of the two yields water.

God's stated formula for renewal, restoration, and revival is quite similar. Man might conceivably pray forever and yet not gain his desired end; the reason being that he has performed only one part of the prescribed two-part formula. But let him add to his praying turning (repentance) and God's promised "then" will certainly emerge.

I note that the prophet Isaiah says nearly the same thing. *"And when ye spread forth your hands, I will hide mine eyes from you; yea when ye make many prayers, I will not hear: your hands are full of blood" Isaiah 1:15.* In that last phrase is hidden the reason for God not answering. There was sin without repentance.

Quick on the heels of his penetrating pronouncement, Isaiah prescribed the remedy. *"Wash you, make you clean; put away the evil of your doings from before mine eyes: cease to do evil. Learn to do well; seek judgment, relieve the oppressed, judge the fatherless, plead for the widow" vs. 16-17.* All of this is repentance in action.

It is for these reasons that agents of repentance are so vital, perhaps far more vital than we might have guessed, for until men really grasp both the need for and the meaning of repentance, it is doubtful they will practice it.

Yes, repentance is of superior consequence. It is really a life and death matter, as the verse at this chapter's head shows: *"...turn ye, turn ye from your evil ways, for why will ye die, O house of Israel?"*

Now let us turn our attention from the means to the end; or as we have already seen, from the "if" to the "then".

"Then I will hear from heaven." It can be assumed with certainty that until there is repentance, God's ear is blocked. His hearing is obstructed by our sinning. To say that He cannot hear would perhaps mislead, but to say that He will not hear is to state the case accurately.

"Behold, the Lord's hand is not shortened, that it cannot save; neither his ear heavy, that it cannot hear: But your iniquities have separated between you and your God, and your sins have hid his face from you, that he will not hear" Isaiah 59:1-2. There is no doubt that when man begins repenting, God begins listening.

"And will forgive their sin." God desires to so totally forgive our sins, that He has made all the necessary arrangements to permit His doing it. In the Old Testament, the tabernacle with its multiplicity of ceremonies and sacrifices provided the means of forgiveness until the "Seed" should come. Thereafter God provided His own Son to take away the sin of the world by the shedding of His blood. Now, John tells us that *"If we confess our sins, he is faithful and just to forgive us our sins, and to cleanse us from all unrighteousness"* 1 John 1:9.

"I will heal their land." When there is individual repentance, there is individual forgiveness; but when God's people, as a body, repent, there is at least hope for a revival of spiritual life on a far broader scale, even to the point of affecting the whole nation.

CHAPTER SIX

REPENTANCE AND CONSEQUENCES

> *Repentance turned the tide for David; yet it could not elimi-nate all of the consequences of his sin. They would come as certainly as day follows night. Nor does repentance nullify the law of sowing and reaping. Surely no one knew that better than David.*

Karla Faye Tucker, the Texas pickax murderess, was executed in Huntsville Tuesday, February 3, 1998. She had begun taking drugs at age 9 and was pushed into prostitution by her own mother at 14.

While yet in her teens she had been a groupie with the Allman Brothers Band and had become a heroin addict. By age 23 she had been married and divorced, and had decided "to give in to her wild side."

On June 13, 1983 she and a boy friend named Daniel Garrett broke into an apartment in the predawn hours, and before the ordeal was over she had heaved a pickax into the chest of Deborah Thornton, a 32-year old guest in the home. Also slain was Jerry Lynn Dean, 27, of Houston.

Both Tucker and Garrett were subsequently captured and sentenced to die.

Albeit, while in prison Tucker was soundly converted. She gave every evidence of genuine repentance and became a remarkably shining light to her fellow prisoners.

As the time of her scheduled execution neared, many who learned of her plight, including such nationally known figures as the Rev. Pat Robertson and the Rev. Jerry Falwell, sought clemency for her, but to no avail. She paid for her crime with her life.

Had she truly repented? Yes. Had God forgiven her? Yes. Could all of that prevent her bearing the physical consequences of her sin? No.

Sinning can set wheels turning that repentance can't stop. While it is certain that repentance is the doorway for clearing accounts with God, it is also certain that repentance may not be the doorway to clearing some accounts with men. Repentance opens God's ears, but it may not shut off man's consequences.

To represent repentance as a cure-all for sin's consequences is to misrepresent the truth. Nevertheless, repentance assuredly does open the door to right relationship with God. And it also does bring God's enablement into the life of the repentant so he can cope with consequences of past sins.

David's life teaches some profound lessons on repentance. If we have a mind and a heart to learn the pertinent truths on the subject, there is no better authority to teach us. Someone has astutely observed: *"Any fool can learn from his own mistakes, but it takes a wise man to learn from the mistakes of others."* Let's allow David to teach us.

Whether a man repents or not, sin does bear its own fruit. But the man who does repent has a distinct and sizable advantage over one who chooses not to repent. King David's experience profoundly illustrates my point.

Few have sinned more grievously that he. From his rooftop vantage point, he saw Bathsheba, wife of one of his military leaders, bathing.

"And it came to pass in an eveningtide, that David arose from off his bed, and walked upon the roof of the king's house: and from the roof he saw a woman washing herself; and the woman was very beautiful to look upon" 2 Samuel 11:2.

Rather than immediately closing his eyes to the temptation, he lusted after her and had her brought to his quarters. He committed adultery with her and she conceived. *"And the woman conceived, and sent and told David, and said, I am with child" (vs. 5).*

Now sin was on the roll. David lost no time trying to cover his tracks. Under the guise of seeking information on how the war with the Amalekites was progressing, he directed Joab, general of his army, to dispatch Bathsheba's husband, Uriah, with an update. But that was only a subtle ploy for getting Uriah home so he could cohabit with his wife and thus make it appear that she was pregnant by him instead of by David himself.

However, David's scheme backfired. When Uriah, obviously a man of highest integrity, forewent sleeping with his wife, David was not a little frustrated.

"But Uriah slept at the door of the king's house with all the servants of his lord, and went not down to his house. And when they had told

David, saying, Uriah went not down unto his house, David said unto Uriah, Camest thou not from thy journey? Why then didst thou not go down unto thine house? And Uriah said unto David, The ark, and Israel, and Judah, abide in tents; and my lord Joab, and the servants of my lord, are encamped in the open fields; shall I then go into mine house, to eat and to drink, and to lie with my wife? as thou livest, and as thy soul liveth, I will not do this thing" 2 Samuel 11:9-11.

Nevertheless, David, now a victim of the irrationality spawned by his sin, would not be outdone or deterred. Sin and Satan are not easily dispelled once they are given an audience or are permitted an entrance. Therefore unwilling to face his failure, and in yet another attempt to cover his devious activity, he instructed Joab, the general of his army, to *"Set ye Uriah in the forefront of the hottest battle...that he may be smitten and die"* 2 Samuel 11:15. Thus David hoped to find a way of escape from the dilemma he had created for himself and to hide his adulterous act.

And just as he had hoped, Uriah died in the battle. Without doubt, David was greatly relieved when Joab sent the "good news." *"Thy servant Uriah the Hittite is dead"* 2 Samuel 11:21. For now the stage was set for him to bring Bathsheba into his own house without being suspected of his behind-the-scene's evil involvement. The only problem was that sin had blinded his eyes to one very important factor. *"...there is nothing covered, that shall not be revealed; and hid, that shall not be known"* Matthew 10:26.

Although the New Testament had not yet been written, surely David knew that eternal truth. Yet he had sold out to his own lust and had become the willing victim of his own passion. He was guilty and God knew it.

Thankfully God fully knows. *"Neither is there any creature that is not manifest in his sight: but **all things** are naked and opened unto the eyes of him with whom we have to do"* Hebrews 4:13. Did He not know, and care, man would no doubt plunge on in his evil ways and find himself damned eternally.

God cared for David. Therefore He dispatched His prophet, His agent of repentance, Nathan. Nor did He send him to act purely on his own. He equipped him with a special enablement, and with a "word of knowledge" pertinent to the case. Before Nathan ever confronted David, Nathan knew what he had done and he knew exactly what to say to jar him back into his own good senses And that is exactly what he did.

"And the Lord sent Nathan unto David. and he came unto him, and said unto him, There were two men in one city; the one rich, and the other poor. The rich man had exceeding many flocks and herds: But the poor man had nothing, save one little ewe lamb, which he had bought and nourished up: and it grew up together with him, and with his children; it did eat of his own meat, and drank of his own cup, and lay in his bosom, and was unto him as a daughter. And there came a traveller unto the rich man, and he spared to take of his own flock and of his own herd, to dress for the wayfaring man that was come unto him; but took the poor man's lamb, and dressed it for the man that was come to him. And David's anger was greatly kindled against the man; and he said to Nathan, As the Lord liveth, the man that hath done this thing shall surely die; And he shall restore the lamb fourfold, because he did this thing and because he had no pity. And Nathan said to David, Thou art the man" 2 Samuel 12:1-7.*

Entrapment is the word. *"Thou art the man!"*

Repentance does not often happen until men are trapped, until they come face-to-face with their own sinful condition. They remain much like their progenitors, who after they had sinned, sought to hide their transgression from the All-Seeing-Eye by their own self-devised covering of fig leaves. However, "fig leaves" are no match for that penetrating eye of the Holy Spirit. For, *"When he (*the Holy Spirit) *is come, he will reprove the world of sin, and of righteousness, and of judgment"* John 16:8.

Even so, we dare not overlook the means whereby the Holy Spirit's work of discovery and conviction is intended to happen. Generally it does not happen apart from an agent—that is, a believer—but through an agent, as in the case of Nathan and David. Had Nathan not carried out his assigned responsibility as God's agent of exposure and conviction, we wonder if David would ever have repented. And we ought not overlook the supernatural element in the process.

Once confronted with undeniable reality, David, perhaps to his eternal credit, broke. Yes, he could have continued his facade of denial and excuse. He could have had the truth-telling prophet executed. And he could have plunged madly on in his sin. But he didn't. No doubt this is an evidence that he was *"indeed a man after God's own heart"* as recorded in *Acts 13:22. "I have found David, the son of Jesse; a man after mine own heart, which shall fulfill all my will."* For once confronted with his sin, he chose to lay aside his own stubborn will, and in its stead to bow to the will of God. That is true repentance.

"And David said unto Nathan, I have sinned against the Lord" 2 Samuel 12:13. What a grand milestone! What a notable turning point! What wholehearted repentance! And what an immediate response it brought from Nathan, *"The Lord also hath put away thy sin; thou shalt not die" (vs. 13).*

The law had said, *"And the man that committeth adultery with another man's wife, even he that committeth adultery with his neighbor's wife, the adulterer and the adulteress shall surely be put to death"* Leviticus 20:10. Nevertheless it is obvious that David's wholehearted repentance had opened the door to God's description-defying grace. *"...where sin abounded, grace did much more abound"* Romans 5:6.

Repentance turned the tide for David; yet it could not eliminate all of the consequences of his sin. They would come as certainly as night follows day. Nor does repentance nullify the law of sowing and reaping. Surely no one knew that better than David.

For our own sakes, as well as for the sake of others, we ought to take careful note of the fruit of David's already forgiven sin. Let it be fair warning to us and let none deliberately by-pass or rashly reject it.

In his excellent devotional, *Pathways to Peace*, Pastor R. D. Ross, a very dear friend of mine, wrote, "Sometime ago a man realized a lifelong ambition when he purchased a very fine barometer. But, when the instrument was delivered, he found to his great disappointment that it seemed to be defective. The needle was stuck. It pointed to 'hurricane". After trying again and again to shake the needle loose, the man sat down and wrote a scorching letter to the store from which he had purchased it. The next morning on the way to his office in New York City, he mailed the letter.

"That evening he returned to his Long Island home. To his amazement, both the barometer and his entire house were missing. The barometer had not malfunctioned. The needle was right. The barometer had warned him of the hurricane, but he paid no attention to it."[10]

Let David's fearful experience of sin's certain consequences, toward which we will now turn our attention, alert us to sin's absolute folly, whether it is graciously forgiven through repentance, or whether its practice continues.

Look at the record. David's illegitimate son by Bathsheba died, despite all of his valiant efforts including fasting, pleading, praying. It was an unavoidable consequence of his own wickedness. It was the abundant fruit of his evil planting. *"Howbeit, because by this deed thou hast given great occasion to the enemies of the Lord to blaspheme, the child also that is born unto thee shall die"* 2 *Samuel 12:14.* Could it be that God was by this means signaling all men, including his enemies, that He has no truck with evil wherever it is found?

It is noteworthy that to this day David's sin with Bathsheba gives evil men occasion to blaspheme. A case in point is the widely taunted film, David and Bathsheba.

But the death of the child and the blasphemy of God's enemies was by no means the only result. Hear Nathan's pronouncement. *"Now therefore the sword shall never depart from thine house; because thou hast despised me, and hast taken the wife of Uriah the Hittite to be thy wife. Thus saith the Lord, Behold, I will raise up evil against thee out of thine own house, and I will take thy wives before thine eyes, and give them unto thy neighbour, and he shall lie with thy wives in the sight of this sun. For thou didst it secretly: but I will do this thing before all Israel, and before the sun"* 2 *Samuel 10-12.*

The tale of David's woes, the consequences of his sin, is a sorry one indeed. Exactly as Nathan had prophesied, it came to pass. And David, in the Psalms, unabashedly describes the painful personal reaping for his own folly.

Albeit, because of his unfeigned repentance, there is a remarkably bright side to the story—a tremendous encouragement for every sincere repenter from David's time until now.

After the second World War, great Britain was deeply scared from the bombs which had fallen in profusion upon her landscape. Yet, in spite of the awful devastation, it was reported that beautiful and theretofore unknown species of flowers emerged from the rubble to adorn the countryside.

David's life was like that. His sin, despite his repentance, yielded an awful harvest of consequences. Yet out of that tangled maze came some of the most inspiring, uplifting, encouraging and insightful truth. What book in the whole Bible has blessed more people than the Psalms? What chapter in the Bible has been more often quoted than Psalm 23? What passage has in it more of a challenge for older people than *Psalm 71:17-20?*

"O God, thou hast taught me from my youth: and hitherto have I declared thy wondrous works. Now also when I am old and greyheaded, O God, forsake me not; until I have shewed thy strength unto this generation, and thy power to every one that is to come. Thy righteousness also, O God, is very high, who hast done great things: O God, who is like unto thee! Thou, which hast shewed me great and sore troubles, shalt quicken me again, and shalt bring me up again from the depths of the earth."

Who has not been blessed by *Psalm 103:1-11?*

"Bless the Lord, O my soul: and all that is within me, bless his holy name. Bless the Lord, O my soul, and forget not all his benefits: who forgiveth all thine iniquities; who healeth all thy diseases; who redeemeth thy life from destruction; who crowneth thee with loving kindness and tender mercies; Who satisfieth thy mouth with good things; so that thy youth is renewed like the eagle's. The Lord executeth righteousness and judgment for all that are oppressed. He made known his ways unto Moses, his acts unto the children of Israel. The Lord is merciful and gracious, slow to anger, and plenteous in mercy. He will not always chide: neither will he keep his anger for ever. He hath not dealt with us after our sins; nor rewarded us according to our iniquities. For as the heaven is high above the earth, so great is his mercy toward them that fear him."

Who has not been inspired by *Psalm 107* to call on the Lord out of the midst of life's devastating circumstances? While space will not permit the quoting of the entire Psalm, a single verse quoted four times in it is a profound faith stimulator. *Verses 6, 13, 19, and 28: "Then they cried unto the Lord in their trouble, and he delivered them out of their distresses."*

There is almost no end of inspiration to be drawn from this marvelous book. It is like a sparkling fountain forever pouring forth its refreshing water toward thirsting humanity. It has inspired more songs and choruses and worship than any book we can name, and all the while it has provided man with the profoundest insights into the great heart of our God.

Credit repentance! Apart from David's repentance the Psalms could never have been written. Apart from his repentance he could have been stoned. He could have been eternally lost, and we could have been without a Saviour. Yes, repentance made the difference!

"And he died in a good old age, full of days, riches, and honor" 1 Chronicles 29:28.

CHAPTER SEVEN

REPENTANCE: PLEA OF THE PROPHETS

(Part 1)

> *"Where there is no truth there will be lies and perjury; for false swearing is brought in to confirm lying statements. And when there is no mercy, killing, slaying, and murders will be frequent. And where there is no knowledge of God, no conviction of His omnipresence and omniscience, private offenses, such as stealing, adulteries, etc., will prevail. These, sooner or later, break out, become a flood, and carry all before them. Private stealing will assume the form of a public robbery, and adulteries become fashionable, especially among the higher orders; and suits of criminal conduct render them more public, scandalous, and corrupting. By the examination of witnesses, and reading of infamous letters in a court of justice, people are taught the wiles and stratagems to be used to accomplish these ends, and prevent detection; and also how to avoid those circumstances which have led to the detection of others. Every report of such matters is an experimental lecture on successful debauchery."* [12]   *Adam Clark*

Scarcely an Old Testament prophet can be found who did not echo God's plea for His people to repent. It appears that always and forever they wandered from the safe haven of obedience into the howling wilderness of transgression and destruction. And, likewise, in every generation our merciful and compassionate Heavenly Father has had His agents of repentance pleading for men to turn from their evil and self-destructive ways.

Hence in this chapter and the next we will take somewhat of an overview of the widespread concern of the prophets for the welfare of God's people, Israel, in particular and for mankind in general.

To facilitate our pursuit we will examine the prophet's pleas, beginning with the earliest and ending with the latest.

Interestingly, on the timeline, the prophet Jonah will be considered first. His prophecy is dated at 862 B.C. and the object of his concern was the great city of Nineveh.

His divine directive was *"Arise, go to Nineveh, that great city, and cry against it; for their wickedness is come up before me"* Jonah 1:2. This should remind us that God is not oblivious of sin, wherever it may be found. His concern is not only with sin as it relates to individuals, but with sin as it relates to cities and even to whole nations. God cannot countenance it wherever it is found.

Our own United States are not exempt. At the very time of this writing, the U.S. Senate is debating the fate of its president, William Jefferson Clinton, who by his own depraved behavior has brought his high office and even our nation into disrepute. The deeply troubling aspect of the entire matter is the very evident unconcern of so many, both inside and outside the Senate, who would simply brush the very evident evil behavior under the "rug", and seek to go on as though it never happened.

We must not forget, there will most certainly be a time of reckoning and reaping. Individuals will reap. Cities will reap. Undoubtedly the entire nation will reap. The only hope for any reprieve lies in repentance. God grant that it will occur.

Nineveh was a "great city". Located on the Tigris river, it was one of the most famous cities of the ancient east, being capitol of an exceedingly impressive and powerful kingdom. In the midst of her great splendor she had luxury, wealth, and magnitude. Her population was vast, with more than *"sixscore (120) thousand persons that cannot discern between their right hand and their left hand; and also much cattle"* Jonah 4:1. Yet, as is so often consistent with material prosperity, there was forgetfulness of God, and outright rebellion against the King of Kings and Lord of the nations. Their sin roared in the ears of the Almighty.

To this city God dispatched His agent of repentance, Jonah. Howbeit, He gained His end only after a fearful and near disastrous encounter with the prophet. Yet finally Jonah went with his message.

Certainly it was not the kind of message he wanted to proclaim, but it was the message Nineveh needed to hear. Let it be noted here that often the most needed message is not the most popular message, nor is it a delight for the proclaimer to deliver it. The important thing was that it was God's message, a message from the heart of the compassionate God, a message with a remedial end in view. *"Yet forty days, and Nineveh shall be overthrown."*

It can be stated that the real message, really the message within the message, was *"Repent, repent or else!"*

"So the people of Nineveh believed God" Jonah 3:5. What a line that is. They took God seriously. They acted. They repented. Here is the record: *"So the people of Nineveh believed God, and proclaimed a fast, and put on sackcloth, from the greatest of them even to the least of them. For word came unto the king of Nineveh, and he arose from his throne, and he laid his robe from him, and covered him with sackcloth, and sat in ashes. And he caused it to be proclaimed and published through Nineveh by the decree of the king and his nobles, saying, Let neither man nor beast, herd nor flock, taste any thing: let them not feed, nor drink water: But let man and beast be covered with sackcloth, and cry mightily unto God: yea, let them turn every one from his evil way, and from the violence that is in their hands"* Jonah 3:5-8.

That was national repentance and it got God's attention; a most impressive example for our nation today.

"And God saw their works, that they turned from their evil way; and God repented of the evil, that he had said that he would do unto them; and he did it not" Jonah 4:10

The prophet's plea had most certainly gained its end.

Then there was the prophet Joel. The time was approximately 800 B.C. His prophetic pronouncements had two distinct aspects, one encompassed a present prevailing condition, and the other a distinctly end time condition. The first, the unbearable state of his nation at the time of his writing, was an omen of the state of things in the end time. To these we ought to give our utmost attention.

In the immediate instance the judgment of God had purposefully visited the land. While it was extremely severe, it was God's compassion in action. The author of Hebrews provides perspective when he says, *"For they* (our fathers) *for a few days chastened us after their own pleasure; but he* (that is: God) *for our profit, that we might be partakers of his holiness. Now no chastening for the present seemeth to be joyous, but grievous: nevertheless afterward it yieldeth the peaceable fruit of righteousness unto them that are exercised thereby"* Hebrews 12:10-11.

To bring the debauched and sin-laden people of Judah out of their godlessness, and out of their drunken stupor, *"Awake ye drunkards, and weep" Joel 1:5*, God had decreed a plague upon the land. It was a plague of insects almost defying description.

Quoting from Van-Lennep ("Bible Lands", i.p. 314) W. J. Deane, MA, says of the locust invasion, "The young locusts rapidly attain the size of the common grasshopper, and proceed in one and the same direction first crawling, and at a later period leaping, as they go, devouring every green thing that lies in their path. They advance more slowly than a devouring fire, but the ravages they commit are scarcely inferior or less to be dreaded. Fields of standing wheat and barley, vineyards, mulberry orchards, and groves of olive, fig, and other trees are in a few hours deprived of every green blade and leaf, the very bark being often destroyed. Their voracity is such that, in the neighborhood of Broosa, in the year 1856, an infant, having been left asleep in its cradle under some shady trees, was found not long after, partly devoured by the locusts. The ground over which their devastating hordes have passed at once assumes an appearance of sterility and death.

"Well did the Romans call them the 'burners of the land' which is the literal meaning of our word 'locust'.

"On they move, covering the ground so completely as to hide it from sight, and in such numbers that it often takes three or four days for the mighty host to pass by. When seen at a distance, this swarm of advancing locusts resembles a cloud of dust or sand, reaching a few feet above the ground, as the myriads of insects leap forward. The only thing that arrests their progress is a sudden change of weather; for the cold benumbs them while it lasts.

"They also keep quiet at night, swarming on the bushes and hedges until the morning sun warms them and revives them and enables them to proceed on their devastating march.

They 'have no king' nor leader, yet they falter not, but press on in serried ranks, urged in the same direction by an irresistible impulse, and turn neither to the right hand nor to the left for any sort of obstacle.

"When a wall on a house lies in their way, they climb straight up, going over the roof to the other side, and blindly rush in at the open doors or windows. When they come to water, be it a mere puddle or a river, a lake, or an open sea, they never attempt to go around it, but unhesitatingly leap in and are drowned, and their dead bodies, floating on the surface, form a bridge for their companions to pass over.

"The scourge thus often comes to an end, but it as often happens that the decomposition of millions of insects produces pestilence and death. History records a remarkable instance which occurred in the year 125 before the Christian era. The insects were driven by the wind into the sea in such vast numbers that their bodies, being driven back by the tide upon the land, caused a stench which produced a fearful plague, whereby eighty thousand people perished in Libya, Cyrene, and Egypt."[11]

Thus it was in Judah at the time of Joel's prophecy.

"That which the palmerworm hath left hath the locust eaten; and that which the locust hath left hath the cankerworm eaten; and that which the cankerworm hath left hath the caterpillar eaten. For a nation is come up upon my land, strong, and without number, whose teeth are the teeth of a lion, and he hath the cheek teeth of a great lion. He hath laid my vine waste, and barked my fig tree: he hath made it clean bare, and cast it away; the branches thereof are made white. Be ye ashamed, O ye husbandmen; howl, O ye vinedressers, for the wheat and for the barley; because the harvest of the field is perished. The vine is dried up, and the fig tree languisheth; the pomegranate tree, the palm tree also, and the apple tree, even all the trees of the field, are withered: because joy is withered away from the sons of men" Joel:4,6,7.11.12.

We need to remind ourselves that what happened to Judah was but a harbinger of the fearsome things yet to come, as also set forth by the prophet.

"Blow the trumpet in Zion, and sound an alarm in my holy mountain: let all the inhabitants of the land tremble: for the day of the Lord cometh, for it is nigh at hand; A day of darkness and of gloominess, a day of clouds and of thick darkness, as the morning spread upon the mountains: a great people and a strong; there hath not been ever the like, neither shall be any more after it, even to the years of many generations. A fire devoureth before them; and behind them a flame burneth: the land is as the garden of Eden before them, and behind them a desolate wilderness; yea, and nothing shall escape them. The appearance of them is as the appearance of horses; and as horsemen, so shall they run. Like the noise of chariots on the tops of mountains shall they leap, like the noise of a flame of fire that devoureth the stubble, as a strong people set in battle array. Before their face the people shall be much pained: all faces shall gather blackness. They shall run to and fro in the city; they shall run

upon the wall, they shall climb up upon the houses; they shall enter in at the windows like a thief. The earth shall quake before them; the heavens shall tremble: the sun and the moon shall be dark, and the stars shall withdraw their shining: And the Lord shall utter his voice before his army: for his camp is very great: for he is strong that executeth his word: for the day of the Lord is great and very terrible; and who can abide it? Joel 2:1-11.

What was the solution in Joel's day? What was God's council to the people caught on the horns of the fearful dilemma? It was as it has always been and what it always will be—repent!

"Gird yourselves, and lament, ye priests: howl, ye ministers of the altar: come, lie all night in sackcloth, ye ministers of my God: for the meat offering and the drink offering is withholden from the house of your God. Sanctify ye a fast, call a solemn assembly, gather the elders and all the inhabitants of the land into the house of the Lord your God, and cry unto the Lord" Joel 1:13-14.

Only repentance could turn the tide for them, and only repentance will turn the fierce tide of God's judgment destined to come upon our world, perhaps even in our time. Let us give serious attention to the plea of the prophet.

Following swift on the heels of the prophet Joel came Hosea. His pleading with Israel and Judah began at approximately 785 B.C. and continued for 60 years.

The situation he faced was little different from that confronted by both the prophets who preceded him and by those who succeeded him. At the very outset he was confronted with the pitiful condition, *"for the land hath committed great whoredoms, departing from the Lord"* Hosea 1:2.

Chapter 4 of the prophecy seems to summarize the conditions prevailing at the time. *"Hear the word of the Lord, ye children of Israel: for the Lord hath a controversy with the inhabitants of the land, because there is no truth, nor mercy, nor knowledge of God in the land. By swearing, and lying, and killing, and stealing, and committing adultery, they break out, and blood toucheth blood. Therefore shall the land mourn, and every one that dwelleth therein shall languish, with the beasts of the field, and with the fowls of heaven; yea, the fishes of the sea also shall be taken away. Yet let no man strive, nor reprove another: for thy people are as they that strive with the priest. Therefore shalt thou fall in the day, and the prophet also shall fall with thee in the night, and I will destroy thy mother. My people are destroyed for lack of knowledge: because thou hast rejected knowledge, I will also reject thee, that thou shalt be no priest to me: seeing thou hast forgotten the law of thy God, I will also forget thy children. As they were increased, so they sinned against me: therefore will I change their glory into shame. They eat up the sin of my people, and they set their heart on their iniquity. And there shall be, like people, like priest: and I will punish them for their ways, and reward them their doings." Hosea 4:1-9.*

Adam Clark, writing a century ago about those conditions addressed by Hosea, provided some insights which incredibly fit our worldwide scene, and in particular the prevailing climate in our own land. He says, "The Lord hath...what we should call a lawsuit, in which God is plaintiff, and the Israelites defendants. It is Jehovah versus Israel and Judah.

"But when has God a controversy with any land?— Answer. When there is no truth nor mercy, nor knowledge of God in the land. These refer to the minds of the people. But wherever these righteous principles are wanting, there will soon be a vicious practice...

"Where there is no truth there will be lies and perjury; for false swearing is brought in to confirm lying statements. And when there is no mercy, killing, slaying, and murders will be frequent. And where there is no knowledge of God, no conviction of his omnipresence and omniscience, private offenses, such as stealing, adulteries, etc., will prevail. These, sooner or later, break out, become a flood, and carry all before them. Private stealing will assume the form of a public robbery, and adulteries become fashionable, especially among the higher orders; and suits of criminal conduct render them more public, scandalous, and corrupting. By the examination of witnesses, and reading of infamous letters in a court of justice, people are taught the wiles and stratagems to be used to accomplish these ends, and prevent detection; and also how to avoid those circumstances which have led to the detection of others. Every report of such matters is an experimental lecture on successful debauchery."[12]

When such conditions prevail, what is God's disposition? How does He who is both good and severe (See *Romans 11:22*) react and respond?

"And the pride of Israel doth testify to his face: therefore shall Israel and Ephraim fall in their iniquity; Judas also shall fall with them. They shall go with their flocks and with their herds to seek the Lord; but

they shall not find him; he hat withdrawn himself from them" Hosea 5:56.

Again in *Hosea 5:15* God is to be seen exercising Himself by withdrawing His presence from the scene. *"I will go and return to my place, till they acknowledge their offense, and seek my face: in their affliction they will seek me early."* That is no light thing. What could be more fearsome than to be alone and without God in the world? The absence of His presence is hell indeed.

We need to hear once again the plaintive cry of *Job, (23:8-9)* and to sense the despair accompanying it. *"Behold, I go forward, but he is not there; and backward, but I cannot perceive him: On the left hand, where he doth work, but I cannot behold him; he hideth himself on the right hand, that I cannot see him."*

When that occurs, what can man do? When God has forsaken, and doom is pending, and judgment is on the horizon, what is the answer? The prophet has it. In a word, it is REPENT! Hear his impassioned plea: *"Therefore **turn** thou to thy God: keep mercy and judgment, and wait on thy God continually" Hosea 12:6. "Take with you words, and **turn** to the Lord: say unto him, Take away all iniquity, and receive us graciously: so will we render the calves of our lips" Hosea 14:2.*

Next in line is Isaiah. He can be called the dean of the prophets, for he towered above them all. Not only did he address the peoples of his own time, but he very profoundly projected Messiah's appearance to open the door of mercy for the transgressor. Ussher, the chronologist, dates his prophecies from 760 to 698 B.C.

While, for our purposes it is not expedient to do an intensive investigation of his prophetic pronouncements, I do want to show that, not unlike the other prophets, he too confronted the evils of men and projected the singular remedy—repentance—just as they had.

His prophesying had barely begun when he began painting a scene of the most deplorable prevailing condition. Listen to his graphic description:

"Hear, O heavens, and give ear, O earth: for the Lord hath spoken, I have nourished and brought up children, and they have rebelled against me. The ox knoweth his owner, and the ass his master's crib: but Israel doth not know, my people doth not consider. Ah sinful nation, a people laden with iniquity, a seed of evildoers, children that are corrupters; they have forsaken the Lord, they have provoked the Holy One of

Israel unto anger, they are gone away backward. Why should ye be stricken any more? ye will revolt more and more: the whole head is sick, and the whole heart faint. From the sole of the foot even unto the head there is no soundness in it; but wounds, and bruises, and putrifying sores: they have not been closed, neither bound up, neither mollified with ointment. Your country is desolate, your cities are burned with fire: your land, strangers devour it in your presence, and it is desolate, as overthrown by strangers. And the daughter of Zion is left as a cottage in a vineyard, as a lodge in a garden of cucumbers, as a besieged city. Except the Lord of hosts had left unto us a very small remnant, we should have been as Sodom, and we should have been like unto Gomorrah. Hear the word of the Lord, ye rulers of Sodom; give ear unto the law of our God, ye people of Gomorrah. To what purpose is the multitude of your sacrifices unto me? saith the Lord: I am full of the burnt offerings of rams, and the fat of fed beasts; and I delight not in the blood of bullocks, or of lambs, or of he goats. When ye come to appear before me, who hath required this at your hand, to tread my courts? Bring no more vain oblations; incense is an abomination unto me, the new moons and sabbaths, the calling of assemblies, I cannot away with; it is iniquity, even the solemn meeting. Your new moons and your appointed feasts my soul hateth: they are a trouble unto me; I am weary to bear them. and when ye spread forth your hands, I will hide mine eyes from you: yea, when ye make many prayers, I will not hear: your hands are full of blood" Isaiah 1:2-15.

Worthy of careful note is his unabashed and forthright identification of sin. There was no effort on his part at diminishing it nor at making it less than it was. To do so, as some are doing today, would be to add insult to injury, and to promote sin rather than repentance for sin.

Listen to him again: *"Woe unto them that call evil good, and good evil; that put darkness for light, and light for darkness; that put bitter for sweet, and sweet for bitter! Woe unto them that are wise in their own eyes, and prudent in their own sight! Woe unto them that are mighty to drink wine, and men of strength to mingle strong drink: Which justify the wicked for reward, and take away the righteousness of the righteous from him!"* Isaiah 5:20-23.

In stentorian tones he is saying that sin is sin, regardless of how men may water it down, or how they may attempt to diminish the evil of it by calling it by some other name—faults, lack of proper self-image, lack of self-esteem, etc. *"For all of this,"* he says, "his *anger is not turned away, but his hand is stretched out still" (5:25).*

Yes, God was angry with Israel's sin, and God is angry with our sin. Yet, while there is any hope at all, He seeks through His agents of repentance to turn the tide. Through them He is ever knocking at the door. He is ever attempting to make sin appear as it really is and He is ever desiring that men repent.

Once more hear the impassioned plea of the prophet: *"Woe unto them that seek deep to hide their counsel from the Lord, and their works are in the dark, and they say, Who seeth us? and who knoweth us?" (29:15).*

"Woe to the rebellious children, saith the Lord, that take counsel, but not of me; and that cover with a covering, but not of my spirit, that they may add sin to sin: That walk to go down into Egypt, and have not asked at my mouth; to strengthen themselves in the strength of Pharaoh, and to trust in the shadow of Egypt! Therefore shall the strength of Pharaoh be your shame, and the trust in the the shadow of Egypt your confusion" (30:1-3).

As has been the case in every previous instance, and as will always be the case, there is but a single way out of the dilemma created by sin. It is REPENT!

"For thus saith the Lord God, the Holy One of Israel; In return-ing and rest shall ye be saved; in quietness and in confidence shall be your strength: and ye would not" (30:15).

Returning and repenting are one. They are the answer. And that answer is in man's hand. Israel had the answer, but the prophet says of her *"...and ye would not."* What will our answer be? What will be said of us?

CHAPTER EIGHT

REPENTANCE: PLEA OF THE PROPHETS

> *"How serious is that woe awaiting those who renege on their life and death kind of an assignment. The blood of the souls that perish is laid at their door and charged to their account. They are worthless watchmen, who boast of a high calling, while all the while they convey no message of repentance to the needy sinner, nor endeavor to show the perishing the way of life. "This man the pastor kills; for in being silent, he delivers him over to death."*   Gregory

(Part 2)

In this last look at Old Testament prophets we will begin with Ezekiel. The approximate period of 595-574 B.C. is the range of his prophecy.

At the heart of his plea is his consuming and intense interest in behalf of the agents of repentance. While he, much as his fellow prophets, has deep and genuine distress over God's erring people, he has a particular burden for seeing to it that God's appointed agents of repentance do not lightly treat their sobering responsibility. The sense we derive is that apart from those agents fulfilling their assigned duty there is scant hope for seeing repentance where it is so desperately needed. Surely that is a sobering reminder for us.

As early as chapter 3 of his prophecy, his focus is on those agents.

"When I say unto the wicked, Thou shalt surely die; and thou givest him not warning, nor speakest to warn the wicked from his wicked way, to save his life; the same wicked man shall die in his iniquity; but his blood will I require at thine hand. Yet if thou warn the wicked, and he turn not from his wickedness, nor from his wicked way, he shall die in his iniq-

uity; but thou hast delivered thy soul. Again, When a righteous man doth turn from his righteousness, and commit iniquity, and I lay a stumbling-block before him, he shall die: because thou hast not given him warning, he shall die in his sin, and his righteousness which he hath done shall not be remembered; but his blood will I require at thine hand. Nevertheless if thou warn the righteous man, that the righteous sin not, and he doth not sin, he shall surely live, because he is warned; also thou has delivered thy soul" Ezekiel 3:18-21.

Who then are these agents of repentance? In the prophet's day they were essentially the priests who bore the sacred obligation for the spiritual oversight and leadership of God's people. In our times they are in particular preachers, evangelists, teachers, ministers of the gospel, and those who pastor congregations, from which they derive their livelihood. Also, in a secondary sense, all believers whom the scriptures identify as an holy priesthood; are obligated to act as agents of repentance. Not exempt are parents who ought to be that to their own offspring, men and women in the workplace who are obligated to their fellow workers, and all believers in their own social contacts and communities.

What a sacred obligation all of these have to all men, to warn them and to alert them to their evil ways, and also to make them aware of the pending perdition apart from their repentance.

How serious is that woe awaiting those who renege on their life and death kind of an assignment. The blood of the souls that perish is laid at their door and charged to their account. They are worthless watchmen who boast of an high calling, while all the while they convey no message of repentance to the needy sinner, nor endeavor to show the perishing the way of life. "This man the pastor kills; for in being silent, he delivers him over to death." —Gregory.

Nevertheless it need not be so, for the man who carries out his sacred assignment by doing what he can to warn the wicked has no blood on his hands. Unless the wicked heeds the warning he will perish, but the agent of repentance will live. He has delivered his own soul.

There remains yet another aspect of this matter that must be noted. Sometimes righteous men sin. They also deserve the attention of the watchmen, for if they continue in their sinning they too will certainly perish. *"...he shall die in his sin, and his righteousness which he hath done shall not be remembered" (vs.20).*

Agents of repentance must act in the sinner's behalf and for his good. In doing so they may discover an attitude like David's, when he wrote, *"Let the righteous smite me; it shall be a kindness; and let him reprove me; it shall be an excellent oil" Psalm 141:5.*

They must not close their eyes to the sinner's condition lest he die and they be charged with his blood. Not only does the Old Testament underscore the agent's serious responsibility, but the New Testament underscores it likewise, and unequivocally. *"Brethren, if a man be over-taken in a fault* (that is, a sin), *ye which are spiritual, restore such an one in the spirit of meekness; considering thyself, lest thou also be tempted" Galatians 6:1.*

None of us delight in pointing out other men's sins, but that is no excuse for avoiding our God-assigned responsibility. On a personal level, I recall attending an adult Sunday School class wherein the teacher set forth the idea that in the light of Galatians 6:1, if a brother is seen com-mitting a sin, the brother who becomes aware of it is obligated to attempt his restoration. And if he does not, then he himself may become vulner-able to the very temptation to which his sinning brother has yielded. That sobered me for sure, for I felt I already had adequate temptation to con-tend with. I certainly did not wish to invite more by my own neglect.

Therefore, from that day until this, I have sought to "warn the wicked." No, I do not snoop out sinning saints. But when I am made aware of them by one means or another, I cannot escape the awesome sense of responsibility.

And I have made a gratifying discovery. In those instances wherein I have become aware of a brother overtaken in a sin, and also wherein I have obeyed the Biblical injunction, almost without exception, the outcome has been most rewarding.

Not to warn the sinning righteous man is to become guilty of his blood. To warn him is to set the stage for his escaping his sin, and for freeing oneself of a serious obligation. *"Nevertheless, if thou warn the righteous man, that the righteous sin not, and he doth not sin, he shall surely live, because he is warned; also thou hast delivered thy soul."*

Before moving beyond Ezekiel let us turn our attention to chap-ter 18. In verse 2 the focus is on a common proverb employed by Israel for escaping responsibility for sin. *"The father's have eaten sour grapes, and the children's teeth are set on edge" (vs.2).* The question calling for an answer is, Are the sins and transgressions of parents not only trans-ferred to their children, but are the children also punished for them? Ezekiels's answer is also God's answer. *"Behold, all souls are mine; as the soul of the father so also the soul of the son is mine:"* (but only)—(my addition): *"the soul that sinneth, it shall die"* *(vs. 4).*

Personal responsibility for personal sin is the concern. The natural tendency is to disown responsibility. Adam did it. Eve did it All men attempt it. But personal responsibility for sin is inescapable. Every man is a free moral agent. Excuses and alibis don't work. *"The **soul that sinneth, it** shall die."* *"The son shall not bear the iniquity of the father, neither shall the father bear the iniquity of the son: the righteousness of the righteous shall be upon him, and the wickedness of the wicked shall be upon him."* *(vs. 20)*

Even so, there is a remedy for sin wherever it is found. It is repentance. It is equally available to all men, be they father or son or any other sinner.

"But if the wicked will turn from all his sins that he hath committed, and keep all my statutes, and do that which is lawful and right, he shall surely live, he shall not die. All his transgressions that he hath committed, they shall not be mentioned unto him: in his righteousness that he hath done he shall live. Have I any pleasure at all that the wicked should die? saith the Lord God: and not that he should return from his ways, and live? But when the righteous turneth away from his righteousness, and committeth iniquity, and doeth according to all the abominations that the wicked man doeth, shall he live?" *(vss. 21-24).*

The prophet's plea continues: *"Again, when the wicked man turneth away from his wickedness that he hath committed, and doeth that which is lawful and right, he shall save his soul alive. Because he considereth, and turneth away from all his transgressions that he hath committed, he shall surely live, he shall not die"* *(vss. 27-28).*

Ezekiel's final plea and the plea of Almighty God Himself is: *"Repent, and turn yourselves from all your transgressions; so iniquity shall not be your ruin. Cast away from you all your transgressions, whereby ye have transgressed; and make you a new heart and a new spirit: for why will ye die, O house of Israel? for I have no pleasure in the death of him that dieth, saith the Lord God: wherefore turn yourselves, and live ye"* *(vss. 30-32).*

Jeremiah's concern and plea was little different, as we shall see. The approximate period of his prophecy was 629-588 B.C. Hear his cry toward Israel:

"They say, If a man put away his wife, and she go from him, and

become another man's shall he return unto her again? shall not that land be greatly polluted? but thou hast played the harlot with many lovers; yet return again to me, saith the Lord.... Therefore the showers have been withholden, and there hath been no latter rain; and thou hadst a whore's forehead, thou refusedst to be ashamed" Jeremiah 3:1,3.

"Go and proclaim these words toward the north, and say, Return, thou backsliding Israel, saith the Lord; and I will not cause mine anger to fall upon you: for I am merciful, saith the Lord, and I will not keep anger for ever. Only acknowledge thine iniquity, that thou has transgressed against the Lord thy God... Turn, O backsliding children, saith the Lord; for I am married unto you: and I will take you one of a city, and two of a family, and I will bring you to Zion" (vss. 12-14).

God's passion, and the passion of the prophet are inescapable. It is also as we might suspect, a passion for repentance. Never does God delight in judgment. He has made the terms for pardon and reconciliation so very easy. All He requires is that men acknowledge their iniquity, that they truly repent. But men, it appears, are given to attempting by their own devices to escape their guilt. *"If the prophet had told thee to do some great thing wouldest thou not have done it? How much more when he says, Only acknowledge thy iniquity?" 2 Kings 5:13.*

The message is always the same. It is turn (repent) and live, refuse to repent and die. It applied to Israel as a nation. It applies to the U.S.A. and it applies to us as individuals. There are no exceptions.

"If that nation, against whom I have pronounced, turn from their evil, I will repent of the evil that I thought to do unto them. If it do evil in my sight, that it obey not my voice, then I will repent of the good, wherewith I said I would benefit them" Jeremiah 8:8-10.

Noteworthy is the fact that God's agent of repentance may be the victim of the very people to whom he makes his plea. *"Beloved, think it not strange concerning the fiery trial which is to try you, as though some strange thing happened unto you" 1 Peter 4:12.*

The preacher of repentance will not always be the popular preacher. People very often do not want to hear such a message, and they tend to take it out on the messenger. They reject the message, and some seek to destroy the messenger. How many messengers of repentance have become martyrs for their message?

Jeremiah was no exception. *"Now it came to pass, when Jeremiah had made an end of speaking all that the Lord had commanded him to speak unto all the people, that the priests and the prophets and all*

the people took him, saying, Thou shalt surely die. Why hast thou proph-
esied in the name of the Lord, saying, This house shall be like Shiloh, and
this city shall be desolate without an inhabitant?... This man is worthy to
die; for he hath prophesied against this city, as ye have heard with your
ears" (*26:8,9,11*).

Even so there is a brighter side. Not all men will reject the message. Some will hear and heed. Some will repent and some will rise up
to call the prophet blessed. *"Then said the princes and all the people unto*
the priests and to the prophets; This man is not worthy to die: for he hath
spoken to us in the name of the Lord our God" *(26:16).*

Jeremiah, despite all of the ill treatment which he received, never
lost his passion nor his plea. His final cry unto God was *"Turn thou us*
unto thee, O Lord, and we shall be turned; renew our days as of old. But
thou hast utterly rejected us; thou art very wroth against us"
Lamentations 5:21-22.

Daniel is next in succession. Nor is repentance foreign to him.
His prophecy is dated 570 B.C. His plea might well be called vicarious
repentance, for in Daniel 9 he is seen identifying with Israel's sin as he
makes *"prayer and supplications, with fastings, and sackcloth, and*
ashes" *(vs. 3).* Throughout the prayer *(vss. 3-19)* he is heard identifying
with the sins of his people. Note in verse 5, *"**We** have sinned";* verse 6
Neither have we hearkened unto thy servants the prophets"; verse 8 *"To*
***us** belongeth confusion of face...because **we** have sinned against thee";*
verse 10 *"Neither have **we** obeyed the voice of our God";* verse 13 *"yet*
*made **we** not our prayer before the Lord our God, that **we** might turn from*
***our** iniquities, and understand thy truth";*verse 14 *"for **we** obeyed not his*
voice."

The question arises, Can one man vicariously repent for a whole
nation? Did it happen then? Can it happen now?

Then, Israel was a people and a nation. Although Daniel was an
individual, he was also an integral part of the people and of the nation.
When he prayed and repented, at least in a sense, the people and the
nation prayed and repented. *"He puts shame upon the whole nation from*
the highest to the lowest; and if they will say Amen to his prayer, as it was
fit that they should if they would come in for a share in the benefit of it,
they must all put their hand upon their mouth, and their mouth in the
dust."[13]

At the least Daniel formed a prayer for the whole nation. To the degree the people of the nation made that their own prayer, to that same degree God would answer. Daniel's exemplary prayer set the tone and the example for the entire nation. In that sense it was a vicarious repentance for all of Israel.

But what of today? Can a single individual repent vicariously for the whole church, and for the whole nation? Can a parent repent for his child?

It is doubtful. For while the church is the body of Christ (1 Corinthians 12:27), we as individuals are "members in particular." Repentance is principally a personal matter, a matter for each of the corporate members to attend.

Conceivably, as in the case of Daniel, leadership can form a prayer of repentance for the whole body, but until individual members give their "Amen" there will be no seeing the desired end.

A worthy example is the prayer of repentance of Minister Joe Wright before the Kansas State Senate: "Heavenly Father, we come before You today to ask Your forgiveness and seek Your direction and guidance. We know Your Word says, 'Woe on those who call evil good,' but that's exactly what we have done. We have lost our spiritual equilibrium and perverted our values. We confess that. We have ridiculed the absolute truth of Your Word and called it pluralism.

"We have worshipped other gods and called it multiculturalism. We have endorsed perversion and called it alternate lifestyle. We have exploited the poor and called it lottery. We have neglected the needy and called it self-preservation. We have rewarded laziness and called it welfare. We have killed our unborn children and called it choice. We have shot abortionists and called it justifiable. We have neglected to discipline our children and called it building self-esteem.

"We have abused power and called it political savvy. We have coveted our neighbor's possessions and called it ambition. We have polluted the air with profanity and pornography and called it freedom of expression. We have ridiculed time-honored values of our forefathers and called it enlightenment.

"Search us, O God, and know our hearts today cleanse us from every sin and set us free. Guide and bless these men and women who have been sent here to serve this great state. Grant them the wisdom to rule, and may their decisions direct us to the center of Your will.

"I ask it in the name of Your Son, the Living Savior, Jesus Christ. Amen."

Zechariah, too, made his plea for repentance. His prophecy is estimated to have been given between 520 and 487 B.C. His concern was that the status-quo might be abandoned, and that the like-father-like-son pattern be eliminated, because, as he says, *"The Lord hath been sore displeased with your fathers" Zechariah 1:2.*

Only repentance could produce that sort of change. *"Be ye not as your fathers, unto whom the former prophets have cried, saying, Thus saith the Lord of hosts; Turn ye now from your evil ways, and from your evil doings: but they did not hear, nor hearken unto me, saith the Lord. Your fathers, where are they? and the prophets, do they live for ever?"* (1:4,5).

The message is clear. REPENT NOW! To delay is to miss God's mercy and to forfeit His glory. Clearly repentance was the plea of the prophets.

CHAPTER NINE

Let it be noted here that repentance is ever the road-builder for the Savior's feet. It paves the way for His entrance into the sinner's heart. It prepares the way for man's personal infilling with the Holy Spirit. It makes a smooth path toward spiritual refreshing and renewal. And it develops a high road for the approach of every blessed provision of God's abounding grace.

"THE AXE IS LAID UNTO THE ROOT"

"The first word of the gospel," says J. Edwin Orr, "is unequivocally...repent." Yes, the first word of the gospel is REPENT. The first word of Jesus' public ministry was REPENT. The first word of Peter's answer to the inquiring multitude after Pentecost was REPENT. The first word of God's commandment to all men, according to Paul, was REPENT.

Repentance is an obviously conspicuous and overarching theme of the entire New Testament. It is launched in Matthew 3. It is prominent throughout the gospels. It plays a notable role in The Acts and in the epistles, and it is significantly evident in the messages to the seven churches in the Revelation.

Nearly 700 years prior to John the Baptist's arrival on the scene, Isaiah foretold his coming and his message: *"The voice of him that crieth in the wilderness, Prepare ye the way of the Lord, make straight in the desert a highway for our God" Isaiah 40:3.* Who can doubt that John's assignment was "Preach repentance"?

Additionally Isaiah foresaw the consequences of John's **repentance** emphasis when he announced, *"Every valley shall be exalted, and every mountain and hill shall be made low: and the crooked shall be made straight, and the rough places plain" (40:4).*

What a graphic word picture of the work of repentance! Its readily perceived mission was to eliminate every conceivable obstacle from before the coming Savior's feet as He arrived on the scene to provide salvation for the whole world of lost mankind. Repentance would prepare the way for Him to come, so that in coming He might prepare the way to a glorious and eternal end for them.

Let it be noted here that repentance is ever the road-builder for the Savior's feet. It paves the way for His entrance into the sinner's heart. It prepares the way for man's personal infilling with the Holy Spirit. It makes a smooth path toward spiritual refreshing and renewal. And it develops a high road for the approach of every blessed provision of God's abounding grace.

"REPENT" was John the Baptist's central message and constant theme. *"In those days came John the Baptist, preaching in the wilderness of Judea, and saying, Repent ye..."* Matthew 3:1-2. And the single reason he gave for that injunction was *"for the kingdom of heaven is at hand."* It is crystal clear that there is but one easily identifiable means whereby sin-laden men can prepare for all that is inferred by *"the kingdom of heaven"* including its provisions, its benefits, and its blessings.

According to John, there could be no substitute for repentance. No device of men, not even the time-worn alibi, *"We have Abraham to our father" (vs. 9)* could suffice.

We do well to remember that, for we are tempted to employ similar tactics. We incline toward dependence on our own religious affiliation, upon previous spiritual encounter or experience, or upon works of righteousness which we have done, when we are confronted with the need to repent. Yet nothing can take its place if the God-ordained goal is to be attained. Repentance, and repentance only, is mandated.

Furthermore, the required repentance must not be feigned. It must not be perceived as a mere gimmick for averting or avoiding judgment. Hear John's severe words at this point: *"O generation of vipers, who hath warned you to flee from the wrath to come?"* Matthew 3:7. A mere show of repentance will not do, not even confession of sin and water baptism.

What then is required? The answer was clear then; it is equally clear now. *"Bring forth therefore fruits meet for repentance" (3:8).*

Positive change must come. Lifestyle must show it. Abandon to the will of God must happen. Careless and deliberate sinning must end. Willing turning away from evil must begin. Pleasing God must become top priority.

Nothing less will be acceptable. *"And now also the axe is laid unto the root of the trees..." (3:10).* Where there is no good fruit, there also will be the axe. An axe to the root will put an end to the evil fruit.

Here is a stark lesson for all. Our natural inclination is to strike out at evil fruit. It abounds all about us and we attempt eliminating it, only to discover that the more we try, the more of it appears.

A major problem exists. It is the time-worn tendency to deal with evil fruit, while at the same time giving no attention to the evil root. Once the axe is laid unto the root it will be discovered that the evil fruit will also disappear. Kill the root to eliminate the fruit! Don't just pluck the fruit!

Now, this is not to suggest that no attention be given to evil fruit, for until the fruit is seen for what it is, it is not likely the root will be discovered. It has been thus for me. While I was striving earnestly to deal in my teaching and preaching with evil fruit, I was made keenly aware of the evil root.

Evil fruit abounds. That should not surprise us. Paul told Timothy it would happen: *"This know also, that in the last days perilous times shall come. For men shall be lovers of their own selves, covetous, boasters, proud, blasphemers, disobedient to parents, unthankful, unholy, Without natural affection, trucebreakers, false accusers, incontinent, fierce, despisers of those that are good, Traitors, heady, highminded, lovers of pleasures more than lovers of God; Having a form of godliness, but denying the power thereof: from such turn away. For of this sort are they which creep into houses, and lead captive silly women laden with sins, led away with divers lusts, Ever learning, and never able to come to the knowledge of the truth. Now as Jannes and Jambres withstood Moses, so do these also resist the truth: men of corrupt minds, reprobate concerning the faith"* 2 Timothy 3:1-8.

The fact that evil abounds becomes our greatest challenge. If we can discover the roots of the tree that yields such an harvest of evil fruit, we will be well on our way toward the answer.

Scripture provides the insight. Evil springs from the heart of man. The prophet Jeremiah gets us on track when he says, *"The heart is deceit-*

ful above all things, and desperately wicked: who can know it?"
Jeremiah 17:9. And our Lord Himself affirmed it when He declared,
"For from within, out of the heart of men, proceed evil thoughts, adulter-
ies, fornications, murders, Thefts, covetousness, wickedness, deceit las-
civiousness: an evil eye, blasphemy, pride, foolishness: All these evil
things come from within, and defile the man" Mark 7:21-23.

The heart is the soil in which the roots of evil thrive, and it is
those roots which produce the evil fruit. What are those roots? We desperately need to know so we can lay the axe unto them.

There are essentially three of them: (1) Infidelity, (2) Idolatry,
and (3) Spiritual Adultery. The first reaction to such a list might well be
somewhat negative. We are prone to attribute each of the above to the
ungodly, to out-and-out sinners. Surely we think none of these could
apply to the community of believers. Whoever heard of infidelity in the
family of God? Who can conceive of idolatry within the Church? And
who can imagine spiritual adultery among God's own?

Think with me about each of these "evil roots".

1. **INFIDELITY:** Webster defines it as (1) lack of belief in a
religion, (2) a. unfaithfulness to a moral obligation: disloyalty. b. mari-
tal unfaithfulness or an instance of it. Further, he defines an infidel as one
who is unbelieving. We consider him an infidel who does not believe in
God.

But what is infidelity in the Christian arena? It is outwardly **acting like God is God, while in actual lifestyle and performance acting
like there is no God.** David described it thus, *"The fool hath said in his
heart, there is no God."* Psalm 14:1.

That was an evident problem with the religionists of Jesus' day.
Have you ever wondered why He was so extremely severe with them?
Why did He denounce them so sharply? It seems so out-of-character.
Look at the record in *Matthew 23:13-33.*

> *"But woe unto you, scribes, Pharisees, hypocrites!"* vs. 13.
> *"Woe unto you, scribes, Pharisees, hypocrites!"* vs. 14.
> *"Woe unto you, scribes, Pharisees, hypocrites!"* vs. 15.
> *"Woe unto you, ye blind guides"* vs. 16.
> *"Ye fools and blind"* vs. 17.
> *"Ye fools and blind"* vs. 19.
> *"Woe unto you, scribes and Pharisees, hypocrites!"* vs. 23.
> *"Ye blind guides"* vs. 24.

"Woe unto you, scribes and Pharisees, hypocrites! for ye make clean the outside of the cup and of the platter, but within they are full of extortion and excess" vs. 25.

"Woe unto you, scribes and Pharisees, hypocrites! for ye are like unto whited sepulchers, which indeed appear beautiful outward, but are within full of dead men's bones, and all uncleanness" vs. 27.

"Woe unto you, scribes and Pharisees, hypocrites!" vs. 29.

"Ye serpents, ye generation of vipers!" vs. 33.

What a tirade! What denunciation! What severity! What jolting condemnation!

Howbeit, He had a reason. At its core it was infidelity. Outwardly those whom He addressed put on a show of piety and godliness, while in lifestyle and actual performance they shouted aloud, *"There is no God!"*

Is that not what Isaiah had in mind when he wrote, *"...they say Who seeth us? and who knoweth us?"* *(29:15)*. Ezekiel voiced the same thing: *"...for they say, The Lord seeth us not: the Lord hath forsaken the earth"* *(8:12)*.

What of us? When are we likewise guilty of infidelity?

When, despite our profession, we act like there is no God. On the one hand we may make the appearance of a devout person. We may attend church faithfully. We may worship enthusiastically. We may shout, raise our hands, dance in the aisle, lie prostate, project every semblance of a Spirit-filled Christian. We might even preach in the pulpit, sing in the choir, teach in the Sunday school, served on the church board. But, on the other hand, and at the same time, be saying, *"There is no God,"* by our actions.

We may be indulging in wickedness and uncleanness. We may be engaged in the all too common practice of watching pornography. Perhaps no one knows of it BUT GOD! That is a subtle and evil fruit of the evil root, **Infidelity.** When we are so engaged we are acting like there is no God.

I recall a time when I was preaching with some vehemence against pornography. Though I had not seen it, I denounced it! Then I heard a "voice" saying, "Who are you to preach against pornography? You have never seen it. How can you preach with any authority against it?" While I now believe that idea could have come directly from Satan, I agreed. I thought I had better have a look, and I did.

I went to a local grocery store, not intending to buy a pornographic magazine, but merely to pick one up and have a look What I saw
at first glance so shocked me that I felt contaminated and corrupted. I
replaced the magazine and immediately implored God for cleansing and
forgiveness, and I promised Him I would never again look at pornography. I repented.

In about a month I checked into a motel, a common practice for
me. Usually, by the time a motel room is readied for the next customer it
is thoroughly cleaned and all garbage has been removed. Not this time.
There on a table, in plain sight, lay a pornographic magazine. That had
never happened to me before. What to do?

I could have said, "My wife isn't here. No friend is here to see
me. I am alone." But I knew that was not true. I could have acted like
there was no God, but thankfully I didn't. I placed the magazine in the
waste basket without ever opening it. From that day forward I have not
been tempted with pornography. Yes, God is still God!

A person can become guilty of infidelity by employing deception
in preparing tax reports, by engaging in deviant sexual practices, as
homosexuality and lesbianism, by carrying on hidden trysts with others
than their own mates, by dishonesty and distortion of truth, by consuming alcoholic beverage and drugs, and by a host of other evils, all of
which spring from the evil root, **infidelity.**

2. **IDOLATRY:** Again Webster defines idolatry as "The worship of a physical object as a god; immoderate attachment or devotion to
something." We conceive of it as rendering homage to an image made by
men's hands, or any other object, such as the sun or moon. Yet we scarcely consider the possibility that a form of idolatry might invade and infect
the Christian community, or that we ourselves might be guilty of it.

How then might we define that "Christian idolatry" which is an
evil root, and which, in turn, bears evil fruit? Simply stated, it is **acting
like another than God, is God.** It is, in practice, placing another person
or thing ahead of God. Remember, actions speak more loudly than words,
especially to God. Hear Ezekiel's word to Israel: *"Thus saith the Lord
God; Every man of the house of Israel that setteth up his idols in his
heart, and putteth the stumbling block of his iniquity before his face, and
cometh to the prophet; I the Lord will answer him that cometh according
to the multitude of his idols; That I may take the house of Israel in their
own heart, because they are all estranged from me through their idols"*

Ezekiel 14:4,5.

Paul's description in *Romans 1:21* and *23* is very enlightening as he speaks of those who *"when they knew God, they glorified Him not as God."* Of them also he says, *"And changed the glory of the uncorruptible God into an image made like to corruptible man."* And again, in vs. 25 he says, *"Who changed the truth of God into a lie..."*.

Men can be termed "quick change artists." God never changes, but men change. Paul says, *"They changed."* And Solomon warned, *"...meddle not with them that are given to change"* *Proverbs 24:21.* This is particularly true when God is the concern. Men so easily change from being God-worshippers to being idol-worshippers, and they do it without realizing or recognizing what they are doing. They convert from being "Creator" worshippers to being "creature" worshippers. They... *"worshipped and served the creature more than the Creator"* *Romans 1:25.* They became idolaters, and rendered the homage due only to God to a creature or to creatures.

Just what is that "creature" who holds such sway over them and what is it that assumes the role of God for them? If we can discover what that "creature" is, we will be well on our way to dealing, as we must, with the evil root.

That "creature" is S-E-L-F. Note, it is spelled with capital letters. Worship of the creature, self, is an evil root, not readily recognized or acknowledged, and not easily eradicated. It is perhaps our greatest idolatry. SELF is an extremely subtle god, ever seeking to dethrone God. It was true of Adam. It is equally true of us. Satan's appeal is to SELF. His tempting lie was, *"ye shall be as gods"* *Genesis 3:5.* SELF is the most productive source of evil fruit.

Of special significance is Paul's comments regarding the last days. Heading a rather shocking list of evils, which are to be manifested, is his statement: *"For men shall be lovers of their own SELVES"* *2 Timothy 3:2.* Furthermore, in the list he provided in Romans 1, every sin he named can be traced to SELF. SELF is the god men tend to serve more than any other god; yes, more than the living God. SELF is the major source of problems in our lives, in our homes, in our churches, and in our country. SELF is our idol, our God. SELF is an evil root to which the axe must be laid.

3. **SPIRITUAL ADULTERY:** Most everyone knows what physical adultery is. It is intimate relations with another than one's own mate. It abounds all about us, having reached alarming proportions. It is

certainly the evil fruit of an evil root. From a Biblical perspective it is outright sin. It violates the commandment, *"Thou shalt not commit adultery."* It is a divorce trigger, a home wrecker, and a sorrow begettor. The ultimate penalty is death.

What, then, is spiritual adultery? Such terminology may be totally foreign to you. You may never have heard it, nor had I. Yet it bespeaks a Biblical concept. It is **acting like you are having intimate relationship** (that is: fellowship, union, oneness, koinonia) **with God, while all the while having intimate relationship** (that is: friendship, fellowship, love) **with and for the world.**

It is a major roadblock to what God desires for the Church, and for what He desires to do in our individual lives in particular.

It has long been a recurring problem for God's people. It was a troublesome problem in Israel. The prophets refer to it often. For example, Ezekiel wrote, *"Therefore thus saith the Lord God; Because thou hast forgotten me, and cast me behind thy back, therefore bear thou also thy lewdness and thy whoredoms...they have committed adultery, and blood is in their hands, and with their idols have they committed adultery"* (23:35,37). It is evident that he was not addressing the issue of physical adultery, but rather spiritual adultery—*"with their idols have the committed adultery."* Their idols held front and center stage with them, while they outwardly made a show of pretended intimate relationship with God.

But what of us? In no way can we question God's longing for intimate relationship and oneness with His children. It is His deepest passion profoundly revealed in Jesus' high priestly prayer in *John 17.* Listen to Him: *"...that they may be one as we are"* vs. 11, *"...that they might have my joy fulfilled in themselves"* vs. 13, *"...that thou shouldest keep them from the evil"* vs. 15, *"That they all may be one; as thou Father, art in me, and I in thee, that they also may be one in us..."* vs. 21, *"...that they may be one, even as we are one; I in them, and thou in me, that they may be made perfect in one..."vss. 22,23.*

The same author, John, speaks pointedly to the issue in his first epistle. In addressing the intimacy with God matter, he stated, *"That which we have seen and heard declare we unto you, that ye also may have fellowship* (that is: union, oneness, intimacy, koinonia) *with us: and truly our fellowship is with the Father, and with his Son Jesus Christ. And these things write we unto you that your joy may be full"* 1 John 1:3,4.

We must learn that intimacy with God should be the priority concern of our lives. Anything else is but a cheap substitute. Only that intimacy, that union, that oneness, that koinonia can yield fullness of joy. Nothing else.

Yet Satan is constantly tempting us to spiritual adultery. That is the issue. That is the evil root. Spiritual adultery puts us in violation of our marriage covenant with God. *"Turn, O backsliding children... for I am married unto you..." Jeremiah 3:14.*

The New Testament uses similar terminology. Listen to the Apostle James: *"Ye adulterers and adulteresses, knew ye not that the friendship* (intimacy) *of the world is enmity with God?"* James 4:4. He is speaking expressly about spiritual adultery.

Spiritual adultery is loving the world, that is *"the lust of the flesh, and the lust of the eyes, and the pride of life"* (1 John 2:16) more than loving God. It involves loving its pleasures, its treasures, its pursuits, its parties, and its practices to the exclusion of God. *"If any man love the world, the love of the Father is not in him"* (vs. 15)

And John adds a profound and most helpful insight when he says, *"This then is the message we have heard of him* (God), *and declare unto you, that God is light and in him is no darkness at all" 1 John 1:5.* This God who deeply desires intimacy, union, oneness, harmony, fellowship and koinonia with us has not a trace of sin in Him, no evil root, and no evil fruit.

Then John confronts us with deep reality. *"If we say we have fellowship with him, and walk in darkness, we lie, and do not the truth" 1 John 1:6.* That is, if we act like we have intimate relationship with Him, while we are having intimate relationship with the world, we are deceiving ourselves. We are really robbing ourselves of the fullness of joy He offers us, for lying is no substitute for reality.

All of this brings us to squarely face and confront the real problem. How shall we handle the evil roots with which we must contend? How shall we handle our infidelity, our idolatry, and our spiritual adultery? How can we "lay the axe unto the root"?

The first blow required of the axe is always the same. REPENT! Apart from repentance there is no hope and no help. Nothing else will avail. *"So kill (deaden, deprive of power) the evil desire lurking in your members—those animal impulses and all that is earthy in you that is employed in sin: sexual vice, impurity, sensual appetites, unholy desires, and all greed and covetousness, for that is idolatry (deifying of self and other things instead of God)" Colossians 3:5* Amplified Bible.

Jesus Himself gave us a cue for applying the axe unto the root when he counseled, *"Whosoever will come after me, let him deny himself,* (better translated 'his self'), *and take up his cross, and follow me"* Mark 8:34.

In summary then, laying the axe to the root of infidelity is turning from (repenting for) acting like God is God, while in lifestyle and performance acting like there is no God, to, in every aspect of life, acting like God is truly God.

Laying the axe to the root of idolatry is turning from (repenting for) acting like another than God is God, to living for and worshipping God for who He truly is.

And laying the axe to spiritual adultery is turning away from (repenting for) acting like you are having intimate relationship with God, while at the same time having intimate relationship with the world, to truly having intimate relationship only with God.

That is God's "present truth" for this hour.

"...it was the Lord Jesus Christ Himself who said: "Repent and believe the Gospel." Some immediately react by supposing that this contradicts the 'only believe' of the Christian message. Does 'repent and believe the Gospel' imply that the sinner must do two things to be saved, and not only one? The exhortation is really only one requirement. The instruction: 'Leave LosAngeles and go to London' may sound like two separate but related requests, but it really is only one, for it is quite impossible to go to London without leaving Los Angeles. It is likewise quite impossible to believe truly without really repenting. The difference between true faith and what the Scripture calls false faith is simple: it is the lack of true repentance. Without a doubt, many who seek to win sinners to the Saviour without specifying repentance in their gospel presentation nevertheless hope that true repentance, that mighty change of mind, heart and life, will ensue, rejoicing when it happens. But their disappointment when it does not happen should compel them to re-word their message so that there can be no misunderstanding whatever."

J. Edwin Orr

REPENTANCE AND REBIRTH

Christianity has had no greater and more effective antagonist than Saul of Tarsus. Luke, the physician, says, *"As for Saul, he made havoc of the church, entering into every house, and haling men and women committed them to prison"* Acts 8:3. Again he comments, *"And Saul, yet breathing out threatenings and slaughter against the disciples of the Lord, went unto the high priest" (9:1).*

Saul's own affidavit is: *"And I persecuted this way unto the death, binding and delivering into prisons both men and women. As also the high priest doth bear me witness, and all the estate of the elders: from whom also I received letters unto the brethren, and went to Damascus, to bring them which were there bound unto Jerusalem, for to be punished"* Acts 22:4,5.

"And I said, Lord, they know that I imprisoned and beat in every synagogue them that believed on thee: and when the blood of thy martyr Stephen was shed, I also was standing by, and consenting unto his death, and kept the raiment of them that slew him "(22:19-20).

"I verily thought with myself, that I ought to do many things contrary to the name of Jesus of Nazareth. Which thing I also did in Jerusalem: and many of the saints did I shut up in prison, having received authority from the chief priest; and when they were put to death, I gave my voice against them. And I punished them oft in every synagogue, and compelled them to blaspheme; and being exceedingly mad against them, I persecuted them even unto strange cities" (26:9-11).

What a record! What admissions! What confessions! What evil acts and deeds! How could such an one possibly become the great Apostle Paul, the profoundly effective servant of Christ, the missionary to the Gentiles, and the author of a good share of the New Testament? There is but a single answer—only through repentance and rebirth. How did it happen? What produced so profound a change? Can a similar thing happen today, and, if so, how?

No one can question that Saul was a religious bigot, a fanatic, and a zealot of the first order. Nor can anyone doubt that he was sincere. His witness is *"I thank my God, whom I serve from my forefathers with pure conscience..."* 2 Timothy 1:3. What then turned him around? What affected such a change? What transformed such a viscious opponent of Christianity into such a persuasive proponent?

The answer is repentance and rebirth. Nothing more. Nothing less. Some may be persuaded that it was pure predestination, and that God had sovereignly elected him to become who he became, that he himself had little or nothing to do with it. But let us consider the evidence. Let us open our hearts to understand what happened.

Saul was no pushover. The more Christianity thrived and proliferated, the more he persecuted and resisted. Yet, despite all of his resistance and his "kicking against the pricks", something of significant consequence was occurring. Though severely blinded by his prejudices, his biases, his religious training, his Jewish heritage, and his strong self-will, he was constantly "seeing" Jesus.

I have a hunch he may have literally seen Him when He was only twelve years old. Remember, Saul's father was a devout Jew from Tarsus, who came often to Jerusalem to celebrate the Jewish feasts. I can easily conceive of him accompanying his father to the temple, and of their having a look at the twelve-year-old boy confounding the Jewish leaders.

It also appears possible that Saul was a respondent, along with the vast crowds that gathered outside of the Upper Room on that momentous Day of Pentecost. I think that because there is evidence that being in Jerusalem to celebrate Pentecost was a passion with him. In *Acts 20:16* it is stated that *"...he hasted, it it were possible for him, to be at Jerusalem the day of Pentecost"*, and again in *1 Corinthians 16:8* is his own statement, *"I will tarry at Ephesus until Pentecost."*

But, whether, as I speculate, he may have seen Jesus on the two occasions referenced above, it is certain he "saw" Him manifested in the lives of His followers on numerous other occasions, and in a variety of circumstances. Yet, it appears the more he "saw" Him, the more he vented his rage and unbelief against Him.

He was like a tree blown upon by fierce winds. The more the wind blows the more the tree adapts to the pressure, and the more pressure it bears the more it is able to bear. However, there is a point where a tree can no longer withstand the pressure and it finally breaks.

So it was with Saul. He was on his way to exterminate Christianity in Damascus. He had all the determination he needed. He also had authority from the high priest and Jewish leaders. He would accomplish his goal. He was in dead earnest, and beside all of that he thought he was pleasing God in doing it. That is, until he met Jesus face to face and discovered who He really was, and heard Him say, *"I am Jesus whom thou persecutest: it is hard for thee to kick against the pricks" Acts 9:5.* That was the "wind" he couldn't resist. It broke him. And they led him blinded into Damascus. What he went to Damascus to see—the Damascus Christians apprehended—he never saw. What he in no sense of the word was willing to see, he saw. He saw Jesus for who He indeed really is.

And what was the result? He repented!

His repentance was no little half-hearted, mealy mouth, "I'm sorry," kind of thing. It was a three day affair. It was no doubt an extended period of deepest sorrow and regret. Think of the anguish that he must have experienced as he pondered his past activities in the light of his new discovery. "Jesus is who they said He was. I persecuted his children. I placed them in prison. I raged against them. I voted for Stephen's death. I traveled to distant cities to vent my wrath. Is there any hope for such a sinner as I?"

Little wonder then that he spent three days and nights in mortal agony, and likely on his knees. Little wonder also that he neither ate nor drank. He was so consumed with his own deplorable condition that nothing else mattered. Repentance was his meat and drink. He had *"meat to eat"* that many know not of. Now he was doing *"the will of him that sent me* (him)*"* as Jesus stated it in *John 4:32,34*. Repentance was accomplishing the end for which it was intended.

Little wonder then that he later wrote to the church in Corinth as he did in *2 Corinthians 7:9-10*. We can be sure his own experience is reflected in that passage. Permit me to paraphrase: *"Now I rejoice, not that I was merely made sorry, but that I sorrowed to repentance: for I was made sorry after a godly manner, that I might receive damage in nothing. For godly sorrow worketh repentance to salvation..."*

Repentance brought rebirth to Saul. Repentance will bring rebirth to any and all who will follow suit.

George Brown was a coal-heaver for the Soo Railroad. He lived with his family in the small town of Egeland, North Dakota. In his earlier years he was an ungodly specimen of humanity. At the time of the Great Depression, the bank where he deposited his money went bankrupt. Along with all others who had their funds in that institution, he lost all he had. As he pondered his loss, he became convinced that his banker was responsible and he had made a decision to murder him.

Howbeit, at that very time, and in the providence of God, through a miraculous provision of food for his family, George became acquainted with Christ. He repented and was born anew. His life was literally transformed and instead of becoming a murderer, he became a dedicated witness and soul-winner.

Although he continued faithfully servicing the trains which passed through his town, he was ever bearing witness to the transforming power of Christ. In those days many transients rode the box cars and they would often stop at George's terminal where they would, without fail, receive a witness and a tract or small portion of the New Testament.

Years passed, and George was ever faithful to his calling, seeking to lead men to Christ. Then one day, my brother-in-law, Dr. Ward R. Williams, picked up a hitch-hiker as he traveled in the southern states. In the course of their conversation, my brother-in-law happened to mention that he was from Egeland, North Dakota. The hitch-hiker brightened up and testified that while he was traveling on the railroad cars, he had passed through Egeland. While there, George Brown had shared the gospel with him. As a result he had been born again.

Incidentally, it was George Brown who gave me the first New Testament I ever owned. It was also in his humble home that I was filled with the Holy Spirit.

Repentance had indeed brought rebirth to George Brown.

Now, the question is, What does repentance have to do with rebirth? Why is repentance necessary to rebirth, and what role does it actually play?

Repentance, by itself is not rebirth. But it does clear the way for rebirth. The new birth is a work of God; repentance is an act of man. Repentance is the forerunner to new birth, much as travail is the forerunner to natural birth It can be said that repentance is man's act, making possible God's act.

However, we need to understand that the simple act of believing upon Jesus, by its very nature, may, and often does, constitute repentance. Believing upon Jesus as Savior is itself an act of repentance. It is acknowledging that one is a sinner and that therefore he is needing and accepting what Jesus did for him on the cross as the solution to his problem.

In this light it can be readily understood that the 3000 souls who gladly received Peter's word on the Day of Pentecost, and were baptized to affirm their faith, were truly repentant.

Furthermore, repentance is an attitude, as well as an act, of the heart. It is an invisible act, though it always yields visible fruit. And it can occur very suddenly. Consider what happened at Cornelius' household.

The record indicates that Peter, though an unwitting victim of Jewish exclusivism, was directed by God to go to Cornelius' house. Once there he simply preached Christ to the gathered Gentiles. And while he preached what appears to have been a very short sermon (perhaps only a few minutes long) saying, *"To him give all the prophets witness that through his name whosoever believeth in him shall receive remission of sins" (Acts 10:43), suddenly and without any fanfare whatever "...the Holy Ghost fell on all them which heard the word" (vs. 44).*

Had they heard about repentance? It seems doubtful. Were they aware that they were sinners? Quite evidently. When they heard that Jesus had come and that through Him they could gain forgiveness, did they not believe on Him and by that very act affirm their repentance? Yes, and so genuinely that God was pleased to respond by pouring out the Holy Spirit upon them, even as He had done in Jerusalem on the Day of Pentecost.

J. Edwin Orr, in a paper titled, *The First Word of the Gospel*, provides an additional and helpful insight: "...it was the Lord Jesus Christ Himself who said: 'Repent and believe the Gospel.' Some immediately react by supposing that this contradicts the 'only believe' of the Christian message. Does 'repent and believe the Gospel' imply that the sinner must do two things to be saved, and not only one? The exhortation is really only one requirement. The instruction: 'Leave Los Angeles and go to London' may sound like two separate but related requests, but it really is only one, for it is quite impossible to go to London without leaving Los Angeles. It is likewise quite impossible to believe truly without really repenting. The difference between true faith and what the Scripture calls false faith is simple: it is the lack of true repentance. Without a doubt, many who seek to win sinners to the Saviour without specifying repentance in their gospel presentation nevertheless hope that true repentance, that mighty change of mind, heart and life, will ensue, rejoicing when it happens. But their disappointment when it does not happen should compel them to re-word their message so that there can be no misunderstanding whatever."

In Cornelius' house repentance, rebirth, and baptism in the Holy Spirit had occurred virtually simultaneously.

We conclude, then, that wherever and whenever there has been rebirth, there has also been repentance, even when it may not have been recognized as such. Further, we conclude that there can be no rebirth apart from repentance.

CHAPTER ELEVEN

> *Genuine repentance always yields its own good harvest. If the repentance is real it will speak for itself in the behavior which follows. Thus it should be understood that repentance is the prime requisite to personal Pentecostal experience. That was, in all likelihood, the reason for Peter's direct and positive response, "Repent!," upon being confronted with the urgent inquiry, "Men and brethren, what shall we do?"*

REPENTANCE AND PERSONAL PENTECOST

Have you ever wondered why Peter responded as he did to the inquiring crowd on Pentecost, when they cried, *"Men and brethren, what shall we do?" Acts 2:37.* Why didn't he simply instruct them to pray, or even to fast and pray? Or, why didn't he direct them, as Jesus did His disciples, to *"tarry...in Jerusalem, until ye be endued with power from on high"? Luke 24:49,* or even as He instructed the eleven prior to Pentecost, *"...wait for the promise of the Father, which saith he, ye have heard of me"? Acts 1:4.*

Why the sudden and evidently unequivocal "REPENT"?

Without question, He had good reason. He, himself, was fresh from the Upper Room. He had, only hours earlier, experienced the most monumental encounter with divinity of His whole lifetime. He had likewise so recently been baptized in the Holy Spirit, and, at the same time He had witnessed incredible spiritual phenomenon. He had, with His own two ears, heard the sound like as of a rushing, mighty wind, and also with His own two eyes had seen tongues as of fire dancing on the heads of His fellows. Not only that, but He had experienced the ineffable glory, along with personally speaking with tongues which He had never learned.

Beyond all of that, He had found Himself fearlessly preaching and pouring forth a veritable river of living water toward the assembled multitude. But why His uncompromising emphasis on repentance? Why not some lesser pronouncement: Why not some less emphatic approach? The answer to those questions is of no little consequence.

I am personally quite persuaded that His forthright answer grew out of His own experience. It is of no small importance to see that repentance was, in all likelihood, the dominant activity during the ten days in the Upper Room, and that that repentance also was a prime factor in paving the way for the Pentecostal outpouring of the Holy Spirit. Peter knew it; therefore he preached it. Repentance had led the way to his being filled with the Holy Spirit. Repentance would likewise lead to the multitude's enjoying the same experience. *"Repent...and ye shall receive the gift of the Holy Ghost" Act 2:38.*

Repentance would set the stage. It, like nothing else, would prepare their hearts for receiving.

Genuine repentance always yields its own good harvest. If the repentance is real it will speak for itself in the behavior which follows. Thus it should be understood that repentance is the prime requisite to personal Pentecostal experience. That was, in all likelihood, the reason for Peter's direct and positive response upon being confronted with the urgent inquiry, *"Men and brethren, what shall we do?"*

Some will question *"For what did the 120 in the Upper Room need to repent?"* Did not the fact that they were there indicate that they had already repented? We will answer the last question first. Yes, indeed they had repented. There is no doubt about it. Their personal repentance had brought them into vital relationship with their Lord. But in answer to the first question, we need to understand that repentance is not a once-for-all act. The need for it is as ongoing as man's everlasting tendency to sin. Repentance is almost a lifestyle. We do well to recall our Lord's word to Peter, *"He that is washed needeth not save to wash his feet, but is clean every whit..." John13:10.*

His insightful point was that they had genuinely repented, but that repentance was needed on a daily basis to deal with defilement encountered in their Christian walk.

John addressed the same issue when he wrote, *"My little children, these things write I unto you that ye sin not. And if any man sin, we have an advocate with the Father, Jesus Christ the righteous" 1 John 2:1.*

Think with me for a moment about Simon the sorcerer. The account is in Acts 8 and it states clearly that *"...Simon himself believed, and when he was baptized, he continued with Philip, and wondered, beholding the miracles and signs which were done" (vs. 13).* Who can deny that Simon repented? Repentance is a part of believing, as we have already seen. The fact that he was baptized indicated his true repentance.

But Simon's problem arose over the matter of bringing forth fruit "meet for repentance."

One-time repentance does not guarantee against further need for repentance, certainly not in Simon's case. For a set of circumstances arose which caused him to act and think wrongly. That he acted wrongly was observed by Peter. *"For I perceive that thou art in the gall of bitterness, and in the bond of iniquity." (vs. 23).* He thought wrongly *"...because thou hast thought that the gift of God may be purchased with money" (vs. 22).*

Surely Simon's repenting again was necessary for his forgiveness, and, I might add, for his preparedness to receive the Holy Spirit. Therefore, Peter said to him, *"Repent therefore of this thy wickedness, and pray God, if perhaps the thought of thine heart may be forgiven thee" (vs.22).*

Now let us note that whenever and wherever the Pentecostal experience can happen, then and there it will happen. Repentance clears the way for it to happen. Repentance is *"the axe laid unto the root."*

For what evil root, or evil fruit was repentance required of the 120? Our quest for the answer will be aided substantially by considering the particular circumstances out of which they had barely emerged. The immediate past had been filled with extreme adversity and difficulty. Judas had coldly betrayed their Lord. Peter had, in cowardly fashion, denied Him, and others of His disciples had forsaken Him and fled. Caiaphas had callously and unfairly treated Him Jewish leaders had vigorously insisted on His crucifixion. Pilate had for political advantage yielded to their pressure and had handed Him over to Roman soldiers for execution. And in turn, the soldiers had cruelly nailed Him to a crude wooden cross.

What then might we expect of them? Certainly all of this and more must have left its mark on not only the eleven, but upon all of those who had made their way to the Upper Room.

Prayer led the list of Upper Room activities. *"These all continued with one accord in prayer and supplication, with the women, and Mary the mother of Jesus, and with his brethren" Acts 1:14.*

One accord in prayer inevitably leads to one accord in spirit, because it opens the door for the Holy Spirit to identify any obstructions to that end, thus making possible the unprecedented Pentecostal experience.

Beautifully illustrating this process is a symphonic orchestra. Let us imagine one with 120 participants. It could never come together by accident or coincidence. It is really a major project. Once they have assembled in a single place, the preparation begins.

Always there has to be a director. And there must be a controlling instrument; that is, one to which all the other instruments must be tuned. No performance can take place until all of the instruments are atune to it. That particular instrument is the oboe, which is "a double-reeded woodwind instrument having a conical tube, a nasal tone, and a usual range from B flat below middle C upward for 3 1/2 octaves" (Webster).

When all 120 instruments are tuned to it, obviously they are also atune to each other. Only then are they ready for the symphony.

Once the performance is under way, emotional responses in the audience can run very high. Some such European performances, I have learned, have been so electrifying that strong men have been so moved that they have unashamedly thrown their arms about each other, and ladies have actually fainted.

What happened spiritually in the Upper Room on the day of Pentecost was not too dissimilar. The 120 were assembled in one room. There was no human director, only the Holy Spirit Himself. Also there was no oboe, except God Himself. The Holy Spirit's objective was to bring everyone of the 120 into perfect harmony with the divine "Oboe", no small undertaking for sure. And it appears evident that for most of ten days He strove toward that goal. What is more, He accomplished it, for "...when the day of Pentecost was fully come, they were all with one accord in one place. And suddenly there came a sound from heaven as of a rushing mighty wind, and it filled all the house where they were sitting" Acts 2:1-2.

Doubtless repentance had been part of the "tuning process", perhaps the most prominent part. It is quite obvious that what took place in Acts 1 preceded what occurred in Acts 2. Yet it is very easy to become so enamored with the events of Acts 2 as to not give due attention and thought to what precipitated them.

Not a lot of detail is provided. We do know that they prayed (Acts 1:14). We further know that they tended to some unfinished business (*1:15-26*). Beyond that the best we can do is conjecture. We know with certainty that they did all that was required to bring all 120 of them into perfect one accord. What must that have included?

Referring once again to the foot washing passage in John 13, we hear Jesus say, *"If I then, your Lord and Master, have washed your feet; ye also ought to wash one another's feet. For I have given you an example, that ye should do as I have done" (vss. 14-15).* He was clearly confronting the issue of human relations. It should be noted here that a man's relationship with God is parallel with his relationship with his brother.

During times of great stress, human relations are often stretched to the limit, or even beyond the limit.

That reminds us of Judas, one of Jesus' twelve disciples. He had served as the group's treasurer. He carried the bag! But he had turned traitor. He had betrayed his Lord, and sold him for silver, and in doing so, he had also betrayed them all. Now they were no doubt confronted with the Judas issue. What would they do about it? Would they simply chalk it up to experience and go on? Would they resent him for the rest of their days? Would they hold unforgiveness toward him forevermore? That was no doubt an issue which had to be settled before Pentecost could happen.

How to settle it? That was the question, and, I might say, a similar question confronts each of us as we face the realities and relationships of life.

Another question also arises. Why forgive so evil a person as Judas? Was he not already consigned to eternal perdition? What good could possibly accrue from forgiving him?

There are some answers. Genuine repentance is always productive. While repentance for serious ill-will toward Judas could not provide any benefit for him, it could most certainly provide benefit for the repenters. Forgiveness is commonly of more value to the forgiver than to the forgiven.

But the Judas issue was likely not the only issue to be confronted. We can easily imagine ill-will and unforgiveness toward a whole list of offenders, including such people as Caiaphas, Pilate, the Jewish leaders, the Roman soldiers, and others. Only repentance could clear the air, but often in the midst of such evil circumstances, some find repentance more difficult than others.

Think of Mary, Jesus' own mother. Hers was the greatest loss. Not only had her Savior been slain, but the son of her own womb. She had every reason to hold unforgiveness, yet she too must repent. Do you see what I mean when I say the Holy Spirit had a monumental task during the 10-day waiting period?

And quite likely there was more, perhaps much more.

Relations had been strained between the disciples themselves. They had quite recently argued over who would be the greatest. Luke tell us *"...there arose a reasoning among them, which of them should be the greatest"* *(vs. 9:46)*. No doubt pride had played a role in the confrontation, and it is easy to believe that the Holy Spirit now had called on the guilty to repent.

In the same vein, some of the group had subtly sought to gain advantage over others. *"And James and John, the sons of Zebedee, come unto him, saying, Master, we would that thou shouldest do for us whatsoever we shall desire. And he said unto them, What would ye that I should do for you? They said unto him, Grant unto us that we may sit, one on thy right hand, and the other on thy left hand, in thy glory ... And when the ten heard it, they began to be much displeased with James and John"* Mark 10:35-37,41).

Now, in the Upper Room, the searchlight was on them in earnest. What must they do to purge such selfish ambition? Again and always the answer is repent.

Then, too, there was in all likelihood the problem of bitterness. What is more of an obstruction to receiving the fullness of the Spirit than bitterness? Nearly everyone, and in particular the 120, can easily find reason to be bitter, but none can afford the "luxury". Bitterness, which is the sure fruit of unforgiveness, erects an impenetrable barrier to the Holy Spirit. Recall Peter's word to Simon who indicated his desire to receive the Holy Spirit. *"For I perceive that thou art in the gall of bitterness..."* Acts 8:23. *"Thou hast neither part nor lot in this matter"* *(vs. 21)*.

How, then, can bitterness be eradicated? It is like quack-grass which is the farmer's constant challenge. My father was a diligent farmer in North Dakota. He was always on the lookout for quack-grass, for he knew well that if it got a foothold in his fields it would soon render his land totally unproductive. In fact a whole quarter section of land nearby had fallen victim to the noxious plant. So how did he handle it? As soon as he found a small patch, he attacked it vigorously with his cultivator. His object was to turn the roots up to the sun, knowing that that would certainly kill them and they would spread no further.

Bitterness is much like that quack-grass. Unless it is dealt with immediately, it becomes a very destructive force. The author of Hebrews warns, *"Looking diligently lest any man fail of the grace of God; lest any root of bitterness springing up trouble you, and thereby many be defiled" (vs. 12:15).* What course of action can we take when contending with personal bitterness? What do you suppose the 120 did? Like my father when dealing with the quack-grass invading his fields, it must be turned up to the "Son," that is, it must be dealt with directly by repentance. That is the only sure remedy.

Doubtless, there were even more obstacles which the 120 had to confront, but we can be absolutely certain that they dealt with every one by sincere repentance.

The little phrase at the end of *Acts 2:2* provides the assurance—*"where they were sitting."* Sitting is quite commonly employed in scripture to indicate a finished task. In the book of Hebrews it was said of Jesus, *"But this man, after he had offered one sacrifice for sins for ever, sat down..." (vs. 10:12),* and again in 12:2, *"Looking unto Jesus the author and finisher of our faith; who for the joy that was set before him endured the cross, despising the shame, and is set down at the right hand of the throne of God."*

In the Old Testament Moses is a classic example. In summarizing the erection of the tabernacle, Exodus 40 employs the statement *"as the Lord commanded Moses"* seven times. Then it states, *"So Moses finished the work."* In other words, he sat down. And it was only then that *"a cloud covered the tent of the congregation, and the glory of the Lord filled the tabernacle" (vs. 34).*

In the case of the 120, when the repenting was ended, when the will of God was done, when all righteousness was fulfilled, then it was that the heavens opened and the first Pentecostal outpouring of the Spirit happened.

As certainly, repentance will clear the way for our personal Pentecost.

CHAPTER TWELVE

> *An all too common danger is that we lose the sharp edge of our concern for the future, and thus allow that to dull our concern for the present. Is not that what Peter envisioned when he wrote to those who would be saying, "Where is the promise of his coming? for since the fathers fell asleep, all things continue as they were from the beginning of the creation?" 2 Peter 3:4. Our Lord addressed the same issue when He said, "But and if that servant say in his heart, My Lord delayeth his coming; and shall begin to beat the menservants and maidens, and to eat and drink and to be drunken; The Lord of that servant will come in a day when he looketh not for him...."*

REPENTANCE AND SPIRITUAL RENEWAL

Maintaining spiritual vitality and freshness is a major challenge for every Christian, and for every Christian entity. Every individual believer, every church and Christian organization, every Christian college and university, every facet of the Christian community, is confronted with it. Believers tend to grow cold and indifferent. Christian organizations and denominations tend to lose their fervor, and to abandon their original reason for being. Christian colleges and universities tend to disconnect from their original mission, and to secularize. Every part of Christianity tends to make an evolutionary movement downward. And only rarely are these trends reversed.

Paul zeroed in on this inclination when in addressing the Romans he wrote, *"Because that, when they knew God, they glorified him not as God, neither were they thankful, but became vain in their imaginations, and their foolish heart was darkened. Professing themselves to be wise, they became fools, and changed the glory of the uncorruptible God into an image made like to corruptible man, and to birds, and fourfooted beasts and creeping things. Wherefore God also gave them up..."* Romans 1:21-24.

If history is any criterion for judgment, and we are persuaded that it is, then the downward spiral is almost certainly inevitable, although not totally irreversible.

It is doubtful if anyone can thoughtfully peruse the Old Testament record of Israel's pattern of behavior without becoming painfully aware of her everlasting vacillating. Not only is it frightening, it is demoralizing. It happened so often, and so many times. One king would reign for a season, doing that which was right in the Lord's sight, and thereby fostering spiritual interest and vitality, which, in turn brought peace and plenty and God's blessings. Then his successor would do the very opposite, leading the people into idolatry, and into every evil practice. And finally Israel would come to total spiritual declension and to the resulting judgment of God.

To support what I have stated above about Israel's behavior patterns, look with me at the record in the single book, *2 Chronicles. "And Asa did that which was good and right in the eyes of the Lord his God" (vs. 4:2).*

"So king Rehoboam strengthened himself in Jerusalem, and reigned: for Rehoboam was one and forty years old when he began to reign, and he reigned seventeen years in Jerusalem ... And he did evil, because he prepared not his heart to seek the Lord" (vss. 12:13-14).

"And Jehoshaphat reigned over Judah: he was thirty and five years old when he began to reign, and he reigned twenty and five years in Jerusalem. ...And he walked in the way of Asa his father, and departed not from it, doing that which was right in the sight of the Lord" (vss. 20:31-32).

"Jehoram was thirty and two years old when he began to reign, and he reigned eight years in Jerusalem...and he wrought that which was evil in the eyes of the Lord" (vss. 21:5,6).

"Forty and two years old was Ahaziah when he began to reign, and he reigned one year in Jerusalem....his mother was his counselor to do wickedly. Wherefore he did evil in the sight of the Lord like the house of Ahab" (vss. 22:2-4).

"Joash was seven years old when he began to reign, and he reigned forty years in Jerusalem... And Joash did that which was right in the sight of the Lord all the days of Jehoiada the priest" (vss. 24:1-2).

"Amaziah was twenty and five years old when he began to reign, and he reigned twenty and nine years in Jerusalem... And he did that which was right in the sight of the Lord, but not with a perfect heart"

(vss. 25:1-2).

"Sixteen years old was Uzziah when he began to reign, and he reigned fifty and two years in Jerusalem... And he did that which was right in the sight of the Lord, according to all that his father Amaziah did" *(vss. 26:3-4).*

"Jotham was twenty and five years old when he began to reign, and he reigned sixteen years in Jerusalem... And he did that which was right in the sight of the Lord, according to all that his father Uzziah did: howbeit he entered not into the temple of the Lord. And the people did yet corruptly" *(vss. 27:1,2).*

"Ahaz was twenty years old when he began to reign, and he reigned sixteen years in Jerusalem: but he did not that which was right in the sight of the Lord, like David his father: For he walked in the ways of the kings of Israel, and made also molten images for Baalim" *(vss. 28:1,2).*

"Hezekiah began to reign when he was five and twenty years old and he reigned nine and twenty years in Jerusalem... And he did that which was right in the sight of the Lord, according to all that David his father had done" *(vss. 29:1,2).*

"Manasseh was twelve years old when he began to reign, and reigned fifty and five years in Jerusalem: But did that which was evil in the sight of the Lord, like unto the abominations of the heathen...he wrought much evil in the sight of the Lord, to provoke him to anger" *(vss. 33:1,2,6).*

"Amon was two and twenty years old when he began to reign, and reigned two years in Jerusalem. But he did that which was evil in the sight of the Lord, as did Mannish his father " *(vs.. 33:21,22).*

"Josiah was eight years old when he began to reign, and he reigned in Jerusalem one and thirty years. And he did that which was right in the sight of the Lord, and walked in the ways of David his father, and declined neither to the right hand, nor to the left" *(vs. 34:1,2).*

"Jehoiakim was twenty and five years old when he began to reign, and he reigned eleven years in Jerusalem: and did that which was evil in the sight of the Lord his God" *(vs. 36:5).*

"Jehoiachin was eight years old when he began to reign, and he reigned three months and ten days in Jerusalem: and he did that which was evil in the sight of the Lord" *(vs. 36:9).*

"Zedekiah was one and twenty years old when he began to reign, and reigned eleven years in Jerusalem. And he did that which was evil in the sight of the Lord his God, and humbled not himself before Jeremiah the prophet speaking from the mouth of the Lord" (vs.. 36:11-12).

What a list! What a sorry history! It appears that evil follows good like night follows day. For them the tides of renewal and spiritual refreshing were like the ocean's tides. They came and they went. Even so, Israel was plainly told what they could do to avoid the tides of evil and its fearful consequences.

"Therefore thou shalt keep the commandments of the Lord they God, to walk in his ways, and to fear him. For the Lord they God brought thee into a good land, a land of brooks of water, of fountains and depths that spring out of valleys and hills; A land of wheat, and barley, and vines, and fig trees, and pomegranates; a land of oil olive, and honey; A land wherein thou shalt eat bread without scarceness, thou shalt not lack any thing in it; a land whose stones are iron, and out of whose hills thou mayest dig brass. When thou hast eaten and art full, then thou shalt bless the Lord thy God for the good land which he hath given thee. Beware that thou forget not the Lord thy God, in not keeping his commandments, and his judgments, and his statutes, which I command thee this day: Lest when thou hast eaten and art full, and hast built goodly houses, and dwelt therein; And when thy herds and thy flocks multiply, and thy silver and thy gold is multiplied, and all that thou hast is multiplied; Then thine heart be lifted up, and thou forget the Lord thy God, which brought thee forth out of the land of Egypt, from the house of bondage; Who led thee through that great and terrible wilderness, wherein were fiery serpents, and scorpions, and drought, where there was no water; who brought thee forth water out of the rock of flint; Who fed thee in the wilderness with manna, which thy fathers knew not, that he might humble thee, and that he might prove thee, to do thee good at thy latter end; And thou say in thine heart, My power and the might of mine hand hath gotten me this wealth. But thou shalt remember the Lord thy God: for it is he that giveth thee power to get wealth, that he may establish his covenant which he sware unto thy fathers, as it is this day. And it shall be, if thou do at all forget the Lord thy God, and walk after other gods, and serve them, and worship them, I testify against you this day that ye shall surely perish. As the nations which the Lord destroyeth before your face, so shall ye perish; because ye would not be obedient unto the voice of the Lord your God"

Deuteronomy 8:6-20.

Beyond all of that, if they did utterly fail, the mercy of God still availed if there was true repentance. Solomon's great prayer at the temple dedication stated it so clearly; there was still a way to recovery, renewal and refreshing.

"And if thy people Israel be put to the worse before the enemy, because they have sinned against thee; and shall return and confess thy name, and pray and make supplication before thee in this house; Then hear thou from the heavens, and forgive the sin of thy people Israel, and bring them again unto the land which thou gavest to them and to their fathers. When the heaven is shut up, and there is no rain, because they have sinned against thee; yet if they pray toward this place, and confess thy name, and turn from their sin, when thou dost afflict them; Then hear thou from heaven, and forgive the sin of thy servants, and of thy people Israel, when thou hast taught them the good way, wherein they should walk; and send rain upon thy land, which thou hast given unto they people for an inheritance. If there be dearth in the land, if there be pestilence, if there be blasting, or mildew, locusts, or caterpillars; if their enemies besiege them in the cities of their land; whatsoever sore or whatsoever sickness there be: Then what prayer or what supplication soever shall be made of any man, or of all thy people Israel, when every one shall know his own sore and his own grief, and shall spread forth his hands in this house: Then hear thou from heaven thy dwelling place, and forgive, and render unto every man according unto all his ways, whose heart thou knowest; (for thou only knowest the hearts of the children of men:) That they may fear thee, to walk in they ways, so long as they live in the land which thou gavest unto our fathers" 2 Chronicles 6:24-31.

However, that was Old Testament and that was for Israel. But what about us in the New Testament era? By what means can believers be renewed and refreshed if they have grown cold and or lost their spiritual fervor or moorings?

Paul has the answer: He says, *"Now all these things happened unto them for ensamples: and they are written for our admonition, upon whom the ends of the world are come"* 1 Corinthians 10:11. In other words, his counsel is, "Pay attention to their history, so that yours is not a repeat of theirs. Learn to profit from what happened to them."

Beside that, we have more. We have the New Testament, with its

Spirit directed counsel for recovery, renewal, and refreshing. It is concerned with both the life that now is and with that which is to come. Both are important, for to have spiritual refreshing now is to be prepared for what is to come.

An all too common danger is that we lose the sharp edge of our concern for the future and thus allow that to dull our concern for the present. Is not that what Peter envisioned when he wrote of them who would be saying, *"Where is the promise of his coming? for since the fathers fell asleep, all things continue as they were from the beginning of the creation"* 2 Peter 3:4. *Our Lord addressed the same issue when He said, "But and if that servant say in his heart, My Lord delayeth his coming; and shall begin to beat the menservants and maidens, and to eat and drink, and to be drunken, The Lord of that servant will come in a day when he looketh not for him..."* Luke 12:45,46.

On the other hand, is John's insightful observation, *"And every man that hath this hope in him purifieth himself, even as he is pure"* 1 John 3:3.

And yet again there is Peter's word of alert and admonition: *"...the day of the Lord will come as a thief in the night; in the which the heavens shall pass away with a great noise, and the elements shall melt with fervent heat, the earth also and the works that are therein shall be burned up. Seeing then that all these things shall be dissolved, what manner of persons ought ye to be in all holy conversation and godliness, Looking for and hasting unto the coming of the day of God, wherein the heavens being on fire shall be dissolved, and the elements shall melt with fervent heat? Nevertheless we, according to his promise, look for new heavens and a new earth, wherein dwelleth righteousness. Wherefore, beloved, seeing that ye look for such things, be diligent that ye may be found of him in peace, without spot, and blameless"* 2 Peter 3:10-14.

The leading thrust is in verse 14, for in it he urges all believers to action and preparedness for a most certain future. Certainly it is a matter deserving more than mere casual and occasional attention. His word is "be diligent." Diligent is the translation for the original "hasten." The idea is, apply yourself with purpose and immediacy.

Some things are top priority. Others are of less consequence, for their scope is merely time related. Those bearing on eternity really matter, but that does not diminish the importance of those which are time-related. Both are of no small significance, and both center on man's relationship to his Lord. Attention is directed to three essential areas of concern.

1. <u>Peace with God:</u> This most important imperative can only be the result of the other two requirements. Until the other two are properly attended, the first cannot be attained. <u>Repentance</u> plays the lead role in obtaining spotlessness and blamelessness, and ultimately peace with God.

2. <u>Spotlessness:</u> What an assignment that is! We need to discover what it means, what is involved.

It means having no blemish of sin, no moral impurity, no sinful impediment. Who then can reach such a lofty goal? Who can qualify, and how? In a world so saturated with sin and evil, how can anyone achieve spotlessness? Yet what seems so humanly impossible must be attained. And time is of the essence. George Barna, highly respected author and pollster, has made the shocking observation that if we don't have a revival of true Christianity in the next five years, the church as we now know it will pass away. Men need to deal with their spots now!

Thank God, there is a way. Yes, there is a way to obtain spotlessness. Jesus said, *"I am the way"* (*John 14:6*). Scripture shows the way.

Jesus, the <u>spotless One,</u> offered Himself freely, so that the <u>spotted ones</u> could become the <u>spotless ones.</u> His blood is the only effective "spot remover", the only sufficient cleansing agent. For *"...Christ also loved the church, and gave himself for it; That he might sanctify and cleanse it with the washing of water by the word, That he might present it to himself a glorious church, **not having spot** or wrinkle, or any such thing; but that it should be holy and without blemish"* Ephesians 5:25-27.

The only question remaining is *"How do 'spotted men' avail themselves of the <u>spotlessness</u> which is so graciously provided?"*

As always there is but a single answer : *"by **repentance** toward God, and faith toward our Lord Jesus Christ"* Acts 20:21. That is the only way. There is no other. **The axe must be laid unto the root.**

In the article called *"The Room"* by Brian Keith Moore, the author relates the following account which clearly demonstrates the great effectiveness of an attitude of true repentance. "In that place between wakefulness and dreams, I found myself in the room. There were no distinguishing features save for the one wall covered with small index card files. They were like the ones in libraries that list titles by author or subject in alphabetical order. But these files, which stretched from floor to ceiling and right to left as far as the eye could see, had very different headings. As I walked up to the wall of files, the first to catch my attention was one that read, "People I Have Liked." I opened it and began flipping through the cards. I quickly shut it, shocked to realize that I recognized the names written on each one.

And then without being told, I knew exactly where I was. This lifeless room with its small files was a crude catalog system for my entire life. T he actions of my every moment, big and small, in a detail my memory couldn't match.

A sense of wonder and curiosity, mixed with horror, stirred within me as I began randomly opening files and exploring their content. Some brought joy and sweet memories; others a sense of shame and regret so intense that I would look over my shoulder to see if anyone was watching. A file named, "Friends", was next to one marked, "Friends I have Betrayed."

The titles ranged from the common, everyday things to the not-so-common—"Books I Have Read," "Lies I Have Told," "Comfort I Have Given," "Jokes I Have Laughed At." Some were almost hilarious in their exactness: "Things I've Yelled at My Brothers and Sisters." Others I couldn't laugh at: "Things I Have Done in Anger," "Things I Have Muttered Under My Breath at My Parents." I never ceased to be surprised by the contents. Often there were many more cards than I expected. Sometimes fewer than I had hoped.

I was overwhelmed by the sheer volume of the life I had lived. Could it be possible that I had the time in my 17 years to write each of these thousands or millions of cards? But each card confirmed the truth. Each card was written in my own handwriting. Each card was signed with my signature.

When I pulled out the file marked "Songs I Have Listened To", I realized the files grew to contain their contents. The cards were packed tightly, and yet after two or three yards, I hadn't found the end of the file. I shut it, shamed, not so much by the quality of music, but more by the vast amount of time I knew that file represented. When I came to a file marked "Lustful Thoughts", I felt a chill run through my body. I pulled the file out only an inch, not willing to test its size, and drew out a card. I shuddered at its detailed content. I felt sick to think such a moment had been recorded.

A feeling of humiliation and anger ran through my body. One thought dominated my mind: "No one must ever see these cards! No one must ever see this room! I have to destroy them!" In an insane frenzy, I yanked the file out. Its size didn't matter now. I had to empty it and burn the cards. But as I took the file at one end and began pounding it on the floor, I could not dislodge a single card. I became desperate and pulled out a card, only to find it as strong as steel when I tried to tear it.

Defeated and utterly helpless, I returned the file to its slot. Leaning my forehead against the wall, I let out a long, self-pitying sigh. That was when I saw it. The file bore "People I Have Shared the Gospel With". The handle was brighter than those around it, newer, almost unused. I pulled on its handle and a small box not more than three inches long fell into my hands. I could count the cards it contained on one hand.

And then the tears came. I began to weep. Sobs so deep that the hurt started in my stomach and shook through me. I fell on my knees and cried, I cried out of shame, from the overwhelming shame of it all. The rows of file shelves swirled in my tear-filled eyes. No one must ever, ever know of this room. I must lock it up and hide the key.

Then as I looked up through my tears, I saw Him enter the room. No, please, not Him. Not here. Anyone but Jesus. I watched helplessly as He began to open the files and read the cards. I couldn't bear to watch His response. The few times I looked at His face, I saw such sadness that it tore at my heart. He seemed to intuitively go to the worst boxes. Why did He have to read every one?

Finally, He turned and looked at me from across the room. He looked at me with pity in His eyes. But this was a pity that didn't anger me. I dropped my head, covered my face with my hands and began to cry again. He walked over and put His arm around me. He could have said so many things. But He didn't say a word. He just cried with me.

Then He got up and walked back to the wall of files. Starting at one end of the room, He took out a file, and, one by one, began to sign His name over mine on each card. "No!" I shouted, rushing to Him. All I could find to say was "No, no" as I pulled the card from Him. His name shouldn't be on these cards. But there it was, written in red so rich, so dark, so alive. The name of Jesus covered mine. It was written in blood.

He gently took the card back. He smiled a sad smile and began to sign the cards. I don't think I'll ever understand how He did it so quickly, but the next instant it seemed I heard Him close the last file and walk back to my side. He placed His hand on my shoulder and said, "It is finished."

I stood up, and He led me out of the room. There was no lock on its door. There were still cards to be written."[14]

3. <u>Blamelessness:</u> It is defined as guiltless, faultless, irreproachable, unblameable. And remember, it is a precondition to peace with God.

Other scriptures underscore the importance of blamelessness, and along with Peter, relate it to the parousia, that is: the Lord's return. An example is *1 Thessalonians 5:23, "And the very God of peace sanctify you wholly; and I pray God your whole spirit and soul and body be preserved **blameless** unto the coming of our Lord Jesus Christ."*

Like spotlessness, blamelessness is beyond human ability. It, too, can be acquired and maintained only by grace, through repentance and faith. It is acquired initially by that means, and by the same means it is daily maintained. That was Peter's reason for urging diligence and haste. Delay is deadly. Diligence brings its own reward.

"Now you must repent and turn to God so that your sins may be wiped out, that time after time your souls may know the refreshment that comes from the presence of God. Then he will send you Jesus, your long-heralded Christ..." Acts 3:19-20. (Phillips)

CHAPTER THIRTEEN

In this hour of permissiveness and careless lifestyle, sanctification and personal holiness are paid little attention. Hedonism has stolen the limelight, and so much so that worldly pleasure has pre-empted the desire for God's presence. The doctrine that pleasure or happiness is the sole and chief good in life has clouded many a believer's vision, and trapped him in a lifestyle that knows little of sanctification and holiness, and consequently little of God's presence. Even so, the scriptures are clear: "Follow peace with all men, and holiness, without which no man shall see the Lord" Hebrews 12:14.

REPENTANCE, A LIFESTYLE

Repentance is an every day necessity. One-time repentance will bring God into a life, but daily repentance will keep Him there.

Although we have noted this previously, it is worthy of more particular attention, for so much is dependent upon it. Next to the grace of God itself, it is doubtful that anything exceeds the need for daily repentance. The fact is that repentance is what keeps the door to God's grace open. Grace alone can save a man, but for that grace to reach a man, repentance on his part is an absolute necessity.

From the time of earliest man God has sought to impress that truth upon him. When Moses received instructions for erecting the wilderness tabernacle, he was given specific direction: *"See, saith he, that thou make all things according to the pattern shewed to thee in the mount" Hebrews 8:5.* And that instruction was for good reason, that reason being that the tabernacle was to be the "road map" whereby sinful man could gain access to the holy God.

Every step of the way was plainly indicated. The first object to be confronted in man's movement toward God was a brazen altar. Once every year blood sacrifices were made upon it to atone for Israel's sins. The mere act of offering signified acknowledgment of sin and repentance for it.

"For the law having a shadow of good things to come, and not the very image of the things, can never with those sacrifices which they offered year by year continually make the comers thereunto perfect. For then would they not have ceased to be offered? because that the worshippers once purged should have had no more conscience of sins. But in those sacrifices there is a remembrance again made of sins every year" Hebrews 10:1-3.

When Jesus came, shadow gave way to substance. The brazen altar which bespoke judgment for sin, and its blood sacrifices, which indicated atonement for that sin, were replaced by the One who *"...after he had offered one sacrifice for sins forever, sat down on the right hand of God"* (10:12).

Thus the sin issue is eternally settled. But man must avail himself of that settlement via faith and repentance.

Beyond the brazen altar in the courtyard of the tabernacle was a second significant item—a brazen laver. It had more than a yearly function. It had a daily function, for prior to any priest, including the high-priest, entering the tabernacle itself, he had to visit that brazen laver. Why? To cleanse himself of sins daily defilements. Sin must ever be confronted and dealt with before man can enter the presence of God, in whom there is no darkness (sin) at all.

The brass of that laver spoke of judgment for daily difilement, while the water in the laver addressed the issue of cleansing from those defilements. None dared enter the tabernacle without first having visited the brazen laver. *"And he set the laver between the tent of the congregation and the altar, and put water there, to wash withal. And Moses and Aaron and his sons washed their hands and their feet thereat"* Exodus 40:30-31.

The same Jesus who provided atonement for original sin, also provided atonement and cleansing from daily defilement. But to take it for granted and to think it is automatic is to err seriously. It is to deprive oneself of access to the divine presence and to rob oneself of the glory and wonder of that relationship.

For this reason, I say, repentance is to be not only a one-time experience, but it must be a daily practice, a lifestyle.

Jesus addressed this issue when at the first footwashing ceremony he said, *"He that is washed needeth not save to wash his feet..." John 13:10.* The first washing He spoke of was the one-time washing of regeneration, typified by the brazen altar, and the second was the daily washing of sanctification prepictured by the brazen laver.

This, then, directs our attention to the whole matter of sanctification and personal holiness.

In this hour of permissiveness and careless lifestyle, sanctification and personal holiness are paid little attention. Hedonism has stolen the limelight, and so much so that worldly pleasure has preempted the desire for God's presence. The doctrine that pleasure or happiness is the sole and chief good in life has clouded many a believer's vision, and trapped him in a lifestyle that knows little of sanctification and holiness and consequently little of God's presence. Even so the scriptures are clear: *"Follow peace with all men, and holiness, without which no man shall see the Lord" Hebrews 12:14.*

Peace with men leads to peace with God. And holiness leads man into His very presence. Holiness is lifestyle. Sanctification is the process whereby holiness is attained. Sanctification, like repentance, is daily. The Assemblies of God Statement of Fundamental Truths, for example, says, "Sanctification is realized in the believer by recognizing his identification with Christ in His death and recognition, and by faith reckoning <u>daily</u> upon the fact of that union, and by offering every faculty continually to the dominion of the Holy Spirit."

According to James Strong, sanctification is purification or the state of purity. The process of sanctifying involves the idea of setting apart, particularly for a holy purpose.

This is what Jesus had in mind when, in His high-priestly prayer for His followers he prayed, *"Sanctify them through the truth: thy word is truth" John 17:17.* As we have seen, sanctification is a process. In fact it is an on-going process, a daily process, and it is accomplished by means of or application of truth. Paul had the same idea in mind when in speaking of Christ's sacrificial love for the Church, he says, *"That he might sanctify and cleanse it with the washing of water by the word" Ephesians 5:26.* His employment of the term "washing of water" was no doubt a reference to that Old Testament symbolism or shadow indicated by the brazen laver outside the tabernacle entrance where washing occurred daily.

The Word is the means to the end, for not only does it reveal the ever-present need for cleansing, but it shows the way to obtain it. The cleansing agent is the blood of Jesus. The book of Hebrews makes it crystal clear: *"Wherefore Jesus also, that he might sanctify the people with his own blood, suffered without the gate" Hebrews 13:12.* And even though the power of that blood is more than adequate for the cleansing of sin and the sanctifying of the individual, its application is not automatic. This must not be overlooked. The individual needing the sanctifying, the setting apart, and the cleansing really has a lead role to play. He, himself, must act. John tells us how. *"If we confess our sins, he is faithful and just to forgive us our sins, and to cleanse us from all unrighteousness" 1 John 1:9.* Confession is <u>repentance in action,</u> and it alone makes the cleansing (or sanctifying) possible.

A problem tends to arise, however. It is the problem of failure to recognize sin for what it is —the "darkness" which obscures God. Let us not forget that *1 John 1:9* is followed by *1 John 1:10.* Verse ten sets off an alarm: *"If we say that we have not sinned, we make him a liar, and his word is not in us."* The more one has His word in him, the more he is aware of his own sin and sinfulness And the more he is aware of sin and sinfulness, the more he recognizes his need for cleansing.

A pastor I know, whenever he is about to preach, prays, *"Lord, forgive me for my sins. Make me a clean vessel to deliver thy Word."* It was Martin Luther who stated that we sin every day in thought, word and deed. To become conscious of our sinfulness, and to be repentant for it, is to be sanctified.

It is somewhat difficult to differentiate between sanctification and holiness. They are so nearly synonymous. In *2 Corinthians 7:1* Paul writes, *"Having therefore these promises, dearly beloved, let us cleanse ourselves from all filthiness of the flesh and spirit, perfecting holiness in the fear of God."*

Perfecting means accomplishing. Always the desired end, the end to be aimed at and gained, is holiness. While the means to the end is sanctification, sanctification is likewise an end in itself. Again Paul will help us. He says, *"For this is the will of God, even your **sanctification**, that ye should abstain from fornication: That every one of you should know how to possess his vessel in sanctification and honor; Not in the lust of concupiscence, even as the Gentiles which know not God: That no man go beyond and defraud his brother in any matter: because that the Lord* *is the avenger of all such, as we also have forewarned you and testified. For God hath not called us unto uncleanness, but unto* **holiness** *" 1 Thessalonians 4:3-7.*

Of one thing we can be very certain, God expects of us both sanctification and holiness, and that we recognize and practice a lifestyle of repentance that accomplishes both ends. Then we can rejoice, knowing that he (Jesus) is made unto us *"...wisdom, and righteousness, and sanctification, and redemption" 1 Corinthians 1:30.*

CHAPTER FOURTEEN

> *Indeed, God "is longsuffering to usward, not willing that any should perish, but that all should come to repentance"* 2Peter3:9. *Howbeit, the depraved will of man can be so 'set in concrete' as to exhaust the mercy of God until repentance can find no role to play.*

REPENTANCE —ITS LIMITATIONS

Repentance has a long list of pluses to its credit:

It is **bedrock** for all Christian experience.

It is the **starting line** for the Christian walk and race.

It is the **foremost key** to all God has provided and desires for His children.

It is the **doorway** to all that grace makes available.

It is the **harbinger** to times of spiritual refreshing and revival.

It is the **cornerstone** to each person's own spiritual house. (Jesus is the chief Cornerstone to His Body, the Church).

It is the **front door** to forgiveness and salvation.

It is the **God-promised means** for escaping the intrusions of darkness upon our lives.

It is the **golden key** to readiness for being baptized in the Holy Spirit.

It is the **escape hatch** from blood-guiltiness.

It is "the **axe** laid unto the root."

It is the **way** to make straight paths for the Savior's feet.

It is even more. Nevertheless its reach does have some limitations. There are some circumstances which virtually slam the door in the face of repentance, or which render repentance too late.

A case in point is that of Judah's king, Zedekiah. God had dispatched His agent of repentance to him and to his people, but to no avail. The record speaks for itself.

"And he did that which was evil in the sight of the Lord his God, and humbled not himself before Jeremiah the prophet speaking from the mouth of the Lord. And he also rebelled against King Nebuchadnezzar, who had made him swear by God: but he stiffened his neck, and hardened his heart from turning unto the Lord God of Israel. Moreover all the chief of the priests, and the people, transgressed very much after all the abominations of the heathen; and polluted the house of the Lord which he had hallowed in Jerusalem. And the Lord God of their fathers sent to them by his messengers, rising up betimes, and sending; because he had compassion on his people, and on his dwelling place: But they mocked the messengers of God, and despised his words, and misused his prophets, until the wrath of the Lord arose against his people, till there was no remedy" 2 Chronicles 36:12-16.

What fearful and fateful words, *"till there was no remedy."* There is a time, and there are circumstances and conditions which shut the door to the possibility for repentance.

Indeed, God *"is longsuffering to usward, not willing that any should perish, but that all should come to repentance"* 2 Peter 3:9. Howbeit, the depraved will of man can be so "set in concrete" as to exhaust the mercy of God until repentance can find no role to play.

Thus it was with King Zedekiah, and the people of Judah. They consistently mocked God's messengers. They gave no heed to His Word, and they rejected His agents of repentance and mercy, until His patience was exhausted. He had given them every reason and opportunity to repent, to no avail. Finally it was too late. They had determined their own fate. They had arrived at a point of no return. They had sinned away their day of grace. And the axe fell. *"Therefore he brought upon them the king of the Chaldees, who slew their young men with the sword in the house of their sanctuary, and had no compassion upon young man or maiden, old man, or him that stooped for age: he gave them all into his hand"* 2 Chronicles 36:17.

Once the "axe" had fallen, repentance would have been too late. Judgment was loosed and there was no escape.

However, some may reason, that that was an Old Testament occurrence. Things are different in the New Testament era. It is never too late to repent. We shall see.

One thing is certain. Once death has come the opportunity for repentance has ended. *"...it is appointed unto men once to die, but after that the judgment"* Hebrews 9:27. But are there ever circumstances or conditions wherein there is no place for repentance? Is it conceivable or possible that one might sin away his day of grace?

We understand that as far as God is concerned, repentance is available and effective whenever and wherever it is practiced. The problem is not a God-problem. It is a man-problem. God forces none to repent, yet there are some who, despite all the God-ordained efforts to obtain it, will not repent. For them there is no hope.

Think of Judas. The scripture says of him: *"Then Judas, which had betrayed him, when he saw that he was condemned, repented himself, and brought again the thirty pieces of silver to the chief priests and elders" Matthew 27:3.*

"This word (repented himself)...denotes only a change of feeling, a desire that what has been done could be undone; this is not repentance in the Scripture sense; it springs not from love of God, it has not that character which calls for pardon. "Mark (it well)", says St.Chrysostom, 'when it is that he feels remorse. When his sin was completed, and had received an accomplishment. For the devil is like this; he suffers not those who are careless to see the evil before this, lest he whom he has taken should repent. At least, when Jesus was saying so many things, he was not influenced, but when his offence was completed, then repentance came upon him and not then profitably.'"[15]

It is true, he confessed his sin. *"I have sinned" Matthew 27:4.* Even so, it was not confession to God, but to his fellow instigators of the crime. His was not godly sorrow, but that sorrow of the world which manifested itself in self-disgust and vexation. It was the *"sorrow which worketh death" 2 Corinthians 7:10.*

Judas had had his opportunity. He had held the exalted position of apostle and treasurer for our Lord. He had heard the truth from the Master's lips. He had witnessed His miracles first-handed. He had experienced Christ's love personally. Yet he plotted to sell his Lord for silver, and in so doing he sold his own soul. *"For if we sin willfully after that we have received the knowledge of the truth, there remaineth no more sacrifice for sins. But a certain fearful looking for of judgment and fiery indignation, which will devour the adversaries" Hebrews 10:26,27.*

Judas' suicide ended any possibility of repentance.

A minister of my acquaintance was in charge of a business meeting for a small congregation. This particular church had been without a pastor for a period of time and a layman had filled the pulpit. During the time of his service he had polarized the people until the church was divided. Half of the members had walked out.

In time, a church official was invited to moderate a meeting in an effort to settle the matter. When the people came together they separated themselves, half sat on one side of the sanctuary and half on the other.

As the meeting progressed, the layman-pastor sought to dominate it to such an extent that the church official had to require that he speak only when given the floor. Otherwise he was to remain seated.

Finally the meeting ended. The layman-pastor was dismissed and the church was reunited.

But the church official found himself struggling with the fact that he had had to deal so severely with the layman-pastor. He made his concern a matter of earnest prayer, until one day he had a very strange and unusual experience. He said he felt that the Lord spoke to him saying, "There is no use praying further for that man. He has settled his fate."

The official was utterly shocked, for he had never had an experience like it, nor had he ever heard of one who had. Later he learned that from the time of that eventful night until the day of his death (some 40 years later), that the man had never again darkened the door of a church.

It appears he had set his jaw. He had made up his mind. He would go his own way and do his own thing. He would not repent. Therefore there was no remedy.

Perhaps this is what John had in mind when he wrote, *"There is a sin unto death; I do not say that he shall pray for it"* 1 John 5:16. Jeremiah conveyed a similar idea when the Lord said to him, *"Therefore pray not thou for this people, neither lift up a cry or prayer for them: for I will not hear them in the time that they cry unto me for their trouble"* (11:14). *"Then said the Lord unto me, Pray not for this people for their good"* (14:11).

We must also consider Jesus' solemn words in *Mark 3:28,29.* *"Verily I say unto you, All sins shall be forgiven unto the sons of men, and blasphemies wherewith soever they shall blaspheme: But he that shall blaspheme against the Holy Ghost hath never forgiveness, but is in danger of eternal damnation."*

The Amplified Version puts it, *"Truly and solemnly I say to you, all sins will be forgiven the sons of men, and whatever abusive and blasphemous things they utter; But whoever speaks abusively against or maliciously misrepresents the Holy Spirit can never get forgiveness, but is guilty of and is in the grasp of an everlasting trespass."*

Let it be understood that no sinner need despair of forgiveness through fear of having committed the unpardonable sin. For the very fact of his inclination toward repentance reveals that his state of mind has at no time been one of entire enmity, and that he has never so grieved the Holy Spirit that he has been utterly forsaken by Him.

"Many sincere people have been grievously troubled with apprehensions that they had committed the unpardonable sin; but let it be observed that no man who believes the Divine mission of Jesus Christ, ever can commit this sin: therefore let no man's heart fail because of it, from henceforth and forever, Amen."[16]

However, as we see it, it is possible for one to so radically apostatize that he may place himself in damnation's way, and thus preclude the possibility of repentance.

Note carefully Mark's word, "Because they said, He hath an unclean spirit." "This helps us much to the true meaning of this declaration. Our Lord does not here speak of every sin against the Holy Spirit, but of blasphemy against the Holy Spirit. These words of St. Mark point to a sin of the tongue more especially, although not excluding thoughts and deeds against the Holy Spirit. Observe what these scribes and Pharisees did: they cavilled at works manifestly Divine—works wrought by God for the salvation of men, by which he confirmed his faith and truth. Now, when they spake against these, and knowingly and of malice ascribed them to the evil spirit, then they blasphemed against the Holy Ghost, dishonouring God by assigning his power to Satan. What could be more hateful than this? What greater blasphemy could be imagined? And surely they must be guilty of this sin who ascribe the fruits and actions of the Holy Spirit to an impure and unholy source, and so strive to mar his work and to hinder his influence in the hearts of men."[17]

One thing is certain, there is a sin for which there is no forgiveness, and consequently for which repentance (though it appears doubtful it would ever happen in these circumstances) is to no avail.

Finally, consider Esau. The Scriptures warn: *"Lest there be any fornicator, or profane person, as Esau, who for one morsel of meat sold his birthright. For ye know how that afterward, when he would have inherited the blessing, he was rejected: for he found no place of repentance, though he sought it carefully with tears"* Hebrews 12:16-17.

Yes, repentance has some limitations. There is a finality to some actions; There are some things repentance can't recover. Once the birthright is sold, it is sold. It cannot be retrieved. Once certain actions are taken they cannot be undone. Once Judas had sold his Lord he could not unsell Him. Once the Lord has been utterly rejected in the face of personal knowledge and experience *"there remaineth no more sacrifice for sins, But a certain fearful looking for of judgment and fiery indignation, which shall devour the adversaries"* Hebrews 10:26,27.

"For it is impossible for those who were once enlightened, and have tasted of the heavenly gift, and were made partakers of the Holy Ghost, And have tasted the good word of God, and the powers of the world to come, If they shall fall away, to renew them again unto repentance; seeing they crucify to themselves the Son of God afresh, and put him to an open shame." (6:4-6).

There is a point of no return and no repentance. It is that point of complete rejection about which A. J. Hodge wrote when he penned the lines of a song:

> "There's a line that is drawn
>   By rejecting our Lord
> Where the call of the Spirit is lost
>   And you hurry along with the pleasure mad throng—
> Have you counted, have you counted the cost?
> Chorus:
> Have you counted the cost
>   If your soul should be lost
> Though you gain the whole world for your own?
>   Even now it may be that the line you have crossed
> Have you counted, have you counted the cost?"

CHAPTER FIFTEEN

> *"Missing was that blessed early condition of peace and joy Godward which the beginning of the religious life so often witnesses. 'All things were new—Christ was new, the Word a new light, worship a new gift, the world a new realm of beauty, shining in the brightness of its Author; even the man himself was new to himself. Sin was gone, and fear also was gone with it. To love was his all, and he loved everything. The day dawned in joy, and the thoughts of the night were songs in his heart. Then how tender, how teachable!, in his conscience how true!, in his works how dutiful! It was the Divine childhood, as it were, of his faith, and the beauty of childhood was in it. This was his first love; and if all do not remember any precise kind of experience of the kind, they at least remember what so far resembled this as to leave no important distinction.' There was fervor of feeling: a great outgoing of the soul towards Christ; much prayer, and that very real; hearty service; delight in worship—the sabbath, the sanctuary, the sacred service; the avoiding not sin only, but its occasions, the 'hating of the garments spotted by the flesh;' in short, there was a close walk with God. Blessed, blessed time, the primeval Paradise of the soul, the golden age, the leaving of which one might mourn, even as our first parents mourned when they were driven forth from Eden to the thorns and briars of the wilderness."[18]*
>
> Rev. S .Conway.

REPENTANCE AND FIRST LOVE

In light of the Revelation's end-time implications and indications, Paul's exhortation to the Romans is most appropriate: *"And that, knowing the time, that now it is high time to awake out of sleep: for now is our salvation nearer than when we believed. The night is far spent, the day is at hand: let us therefore cast off the works of darkness, and let us put on the armour of light"* (13:11-12).

Paul penned those lines nearly 2000 years ago. If he intended that they be taken seriously then, how much more should we *"upon whom the ends of the worlds are come"* give them our most careful attention?

While Jesus' word to the seven churches no doubt sounded an alarm of great consequence to them then, how much more should they awaken and alert us today?

The message is unmistakably clear. It is what it has ever been— ***"Repent!"*** Five of the seven churches heard it, indicating the near universal need for it. And if those in the Church need it, how much more those outside the Church? *"For the time is come that judgment must begin at the house of God: and if it first begin at us, what shall the end be of them that obey not the gospel of God?"* 1 Peter 4:17.

The Revelation's first message was addressed to the church at Ephesus. It is highly significant for several reasons. That church was founded by none less than the Apostle Paul himself. It had a most impressive beginning. Credit the eloquent Apollos with the first converts to Christianity in the city. Then came Paul. While Apollos was a disciple of John the Baptist, and thus limited in Christian knowledge and experience, Paul came with full knowledge and experience, and with a passion that all men should share what he had.

Therefore he was not about to let the Ephesians come short of what he perceived was available for them. Not only had he led them into the waters of Christian baptism, but he had also laid his hands upon them so that everyone present personally experienced a mighty infilling with the Holy Spirit. Then for two years he was their pastor. He taught them, and he led them by both example and practice in evangelizing not merely their own city, but *"all they which dwelt in Asia."* Certainly it is evident that his own love for Christ, and his passion for lost men was transmitted to them.

Thus began that phenomenal church. But it was by no means its end. That was also the beginning of Paul's concern for the Ephesians, nor was it the end of that concern. For it was to that same church that he, some ten years later, wrote his remarkable epistle.

In that epistle his heartfelt burden is quite evident. Time has a way of eroding concern and passion, and various factors contributed to the erosion, many of which Paul addressed. But at the heart of the epistle is evidence of his chief concern—that the Ephesians might be dominated by their first love. Hear him pray in *Ephesians 3:17, "That Christ may dwell in your hearts by faith; that ye, being rooted and grounded in love, May be able to comprehend with all saints what is the breadth, and* *length, and depth, and height; and to know the **love of Christ**, which pas-seth knowledge, that ye might be filled with all the fulness of God."*

Approximately thirty years later, what had been Paul's great con-cern was now the risen Jesus' overriding concern for the same church. *"Nevertheless I have somewhat against thee, because thou has left thy first love" Revelation 2:4.*

When we, His Church, and as individual members of that Church, become His concern, then it is certainly time that His concern becomes our concern. But does it? Does it concern us that we might have left our first love? And are we vitally interested in doing whatever is nec-essary to remedy the problem?

Before a problem can be remedied, it has to be understood. What was that "grave thing" (as the Greek states it), which the Lord had against them? What did He mean by *"thou hast left thy first love,"* as is expressed even more emphatically with the article repeated: *"thou hast left thy love, thy first love"*?

While, in all likelihood it included their love for each other, and their love for lost men everywhere, yet also in all probability it was their own personal love for Him which had severely sagged and faded. Though they were still following the "letter of the law," so to speak, it was the "spirit of the law" that was wanting.

"Missing was that blessed early condition of peace and joy Godward which the beginning of the religious life so often witnesses. 'All things were new—Christ was new, the Word a new light, worship a new gift, the world a new realm of beauty, shining in the brightness of its Author; even the man himself was new to himself. Sin was gone, and fear also was gone with it. To love was his all, and he loved everything. The day dawned in joy, and the thoughts of the night were songs in his heart. Then how tender, how teachable! in his conscience how true!, in his works how dutiful! It was the Divine childhood, as it were, of his faith, and the beauty of childhood was in it. This was his first love; and if all do not remember any precise kind of experience of the kind, they at least remember what so far resembled this as to leave no important distinc-tion.' There was fervor of feeling: a great outgoing of the soul towards Christ; much prayer, and that very real; hearty service; delight in wor-ship—the sabbath, the sanctuary, the sacred service; the avoiding, not sin only, but its occasions, the 'hating of the garments spotted by the flesh;' in short, there was a close walk with God. Blessed, blessed time, the primeval Paradise of the soul, the golden age, the leaving of which one might mourn, even as our first parents mourned when they were driven

forth from Eden to the thorns and briars of the wilderness."
Rev. S. Conway [18]

All of that was now a thing of the past. Yes, they still knew the routine. They did the works. They labored. They had patience. They despised and, no doubt, condemned those that were evil. They evidently disciplined and even rejected false prophets. They labored and had not fainted. They certainly had a most impressive list of good deeds to their credit.

We would say they were very orthodox and very faithful to the traditions. Much like Martha in John 10, they were *"careful and troubled about many things" (vs. 42)*, but they had neglected the "one thing" that is needful, and in so doing they had incurred the Lord's extreme displeasure. They had left their "first love." "Left" can as well be translated "forsaken" or "laid aside." Thus it appears it was at least an act of careless unconcern, or possibly even a deliberate act.

The question before us is, What course of action could they take to remedy their most despicable and unwarranted action? What new program could they introduce? What new innovation could they adopt? What new form of worship could they acquire? What new formula for spirituality could they set forth, and thereby regain the Lord's approval?

The answer to every question is the same. None! None whatsoever! Nothing they could attempt could suffice. And, I might add, neither can it in our case. But there is an answer. There is a solution for lost first love. However, before we discover it, we will pursue an understanding of what first love really was and is.

First love and first works are nearly synonymous. The Ephesian departure from them appears to have been a contagion. It may have begun with only a few but now it had affected the whole church. A little leaven leavens the whole lump. The truth is, no single member lives to himself, nor does he die to himself. Even a lone person moving in the wrong direction can influence many others, but likewise a lone person can definitely impact many others by moving in the right direction.

Since Jesus gave no definition of first love and first works, it is quite obvious that the Ephesians knew what He meant by the terms. No doubt there is a close parallel between natural relationships and spiritual relationships which will enlarge our understanding. Therefore, if we give attention to the natural we will come to more fully understand the spiritual. The natural is but a shadow of the spiritual. It reflects the spiritual, as when Jesus related spiritual birth to natural birth (See John 3:3-7) and when He related the moving of the Holy Spirit to the wind (3:8).

Comprehending Jesus' employment of first love as He intended is our present concern. Ponder it with me.

In the outset, note that natural first love is enamored with its object. Likewise it is with spiritual first love, whose object is the Lord Himself.

For those in the throes of natural first love, the object of that love is front and center. He (or she) leads the parade. He is the epitome of their admiration, adoration, and affection. For them he is the fairest of the fair. He is the theme of their song, the apple of their eye, and the treasure of their heart. None other, and nothing other, can 'hold a candle' compared to him. He is their all-in-all, their everything. He is what Solomon was to his beloved.

"As the apple tree among the trees of the wood, so is my beloved among the sons. I sat down under his shadow with great delight, and his fruit was sweet to my taste. He brought me to the banqueting house, and his banner over me was love. Stay me with flagons, comfort me with apples: for I am sick of love. His left hand is under my head, and his right hand doth embrace me. I charge you, O ye daughters of Jerusalem, by the roes, and by the hinds of the field, that ye stir not up, nor awake my love, till he please" Song of Solomon 2:3-7.

"My beloved is white and ruddy, the chiefest among ten thousand. His head is as the most fine gold, his locks are bushy, and black as a raven. His eyes are as the eyes of doves by the rivers of waters, washed with milk and fitly set. His cheeks are as a bed of spices, as sweet flowers: his lips like lilies, dropping sweet smelling myrrh. His hands are as pillars of marble, set upon sockets of fine gold: his countenance is as Lebanon, excellent as the cedars. His mouth is most sweet: yea, he is altogether lovely. this is my beloved, and this is my friend, O daughters of Jerusalem" (5:9-16).

That is first love in full bloom.

Further, first love is enraptured with its object's presence and nearness. It cannot countenance departure and separation. Who can better illustrate this than Ruth, the daughter-in-law to Naomi? *"...but Ruth clave unto her. And she said, Behold, thy sister in law is gone back unto her people and unto her gods: return thou after thy sister in law. And Ruth said, Intreat me not to leave thee, or to return from following after thee: for whither thou goest, I will go; and where thou lodgest, I will lodge: thy people shall be my people, and thy God my God: Where thou diest, will I die, and there will I be buried: the Lord do so to me, and more also, if ought but death part thee and me."Ruth 1:14-17.*

Add to that the impassioned cry of Solomon's beloved. *"The watchmen that go about the city found me: to whom I said, Saw ye him whom my soul loveth? It was but a little that I passed from them, but I found him whom my soul loveth: I held him, and would not let him go, until I had brought him into my mother's house" Song of Solomon 5:9-16.*

First love can but scarcely abide separation. For it, presence is equitable with life itself. Yet, evidently the Church at Ephesus had gradually learned to satisfy itself with images of the past, and objects, and performance until these had become substitutes for their Lord's presence, and they no longer discerned the difference.

They had left their first love!

Then too, first love is so <u>enthralled with its object as to be committed to total obedience and submission.</u> Its obedience and submission are not legislated or demanded. They are freely and joyfully given. They are not coerced or required, but they are the spontaneous response of a captivated heart.

Additionally, first love is <u>enchanted with exclusivism.</u> It is single-minded. It has but a single lover. *"I am my beloved's, and my beloved is mine" Song of Solomon 6:3.* First love closes its eyes to any other who may seek to intrude. It gives no place to any other. It is so enthralled as to desire no other.

Moreover, it is <u>engulfed in oneness.</u> Its ultimate expression on the natural plane is conjugal relationship, that relationship which so merges two entities that they become one. *"...for two, saith he, shall be one flesh" 1 Corinthians 6:16.* And this perhaps, best of all, illustrates the tragic loss of first love among the Ephesians. They had been enamored with Him. He had once been the epitomy of their admiration, adoration and affection. He had been the fairest of ten thousand. They had been enraptured with His nearness and presence. They had been committed to complete obedience and total submission. They had been enchanted with exclusivism. He was their single and only love. And they had been engulfed in that blessed oneness which was the passion of His great heart. But now that was no longer the case.

Oh, yes, they no doubt testified of fellowship with Him, of union and oneness and koinonia, and of the most intimate of relationships with Him, but they were walking in darkness. *"If we say we have fellowship*

with him, and walk in darkness, we lie and do not the truth" 1 John 1:6.
Their first love had fallen victim to other loves.

It is dangerously easy to become disenchanted, not because the
object of first love has changed, but because of the ever present allure-
ments of this present world, and the inherent weakness of the flesh with
its passions and lusts.

So what is the case with us as individuals today, and what of the
Church in general? Does first love still burn brightly? Is it the motivation for first works, or have we condescended to substitutes? Are we as
enamored with Jesus as we once were? Is He really the fairest of ten
thousand to us? Or are we much like the man who reportedly told his
lady friend, "I love you so much I'd travel around the world to be with
you." And who then added, "I'll be over to see you tomorrow if it does-
n't rain!"

Are we as enamored with his presence as was once the case? Is
His manifested presence our chief desire, delight and pursuit, or do we
rather relegate that to the past, and go merrily on our way without it, and
without being keenly aware of our loss? When Job was in the bitter
throes of his personal dark and lonely night, his anguished heart-cry was,
*"Behold, I go forward, but he is not there; and backward, but I cannot
perceive him. On the left hand, where he doth work, but I cannot behold
him: he hideth himself on the right hand, that I cannot see him" Job
23:8,9.* Are we like that? Or are we satisfied with memory instead of
reality?

Again, are we so enthralled with our Lord as to be wholly committed to total obedience and submission? Is His will our first and topmost consideration? Is it our priority desire to please Him in all that we
do?

How well do I recall that while I was in my mid-teens I fell in
love with the girl of my dreams, whom I later married, and to whom I
have been wed for more than 60 years. That first love was so intense that
I would have done anything to please her. I learned that she (whether
rightly or wrongly) did not condone reading the "funny paper". And so
in my effort to measure up, I discontinued reading them. Further, I discovered her disapproval of the use of slang, and that ended an established
habit. I would have done anything to gain her approval.

Thus it was with our Lord. His own affidavit was *"...I do always
those things that please him" John 8:29.* And He demonstrated His

absolute commitment when in His most fearful and intense agony in Gethsemane he cried, *"Abba, Father, all things are possible unto thee; take away this cup from me: nevertheless not what I will, but what thou wilt" Mark 14:36.* That is first love epitomized and exemplified.

Once more, what of exclusivism? Does our Lord hold such a place in our lives that no other can intrude? Is He the clear and central focus to the total abandon of all other loves? Is He to us what He was to King David when he cried, *"O God, thou art my God; early will I seek thee: my soul thirsteth for thee, my flesh longeth for thee in a dry and thirsty land, where no water is;To see thy power and thy glory, so as I have seen thee in the sanctuary. Because thy loving kindness is better than life, my lips shall praise thee" Psalm 63:1-3.* Or are we quite indifferent to Him because other loves have robbed Him of that exclusivism which is rightly His?

And, finally, what of our oneness with Him? Are we one in spirit with him, or have we permitted a sort of oneness with the world to rob us of that blessed oneness with the Father, and with His Son? Remember, it was the overriding passion of Jesus that oneness should prevail with His followers. *"And the glory which thou gavest me I have given them; that they may be one, even as we are one: I in them, and thou in me, that they may be perfect in one; and that the world may know that thou hast sent me, and hast loved them, as thou hast loved me" John 17:22,23.*

Certainly it was not oneness with the world that Jesus had in mind, but rather it was oneness in glory, in character, and indeed in nature and in being. It was oneness with that God who is light, and in whom there is no darkness at all. It was union of the highest order. It was genuine koinonia with the Father and the Son. It was total cooperation with His purpose and mission. It was that full agreement in spirit wherein two become one. That is first love and it was that in which the Ephesian church had faulted to the point of incurring our Lord's disfavor and severe warning. It is likewise an area of concern in the Church today. It is our Lord's concern, and it must become ours.

What then is the pathway to recovery: How can that which has been "left" be regained? The Lord provided the only foolproof solution: *"Remember from whence thou art fallen, and repent, and do the first works" Revelation 2:15.* Remember, repent, and do! Three steps which together assure an absolute solution.

Generally a backward look is not considered healthy. But in the case of first love, it has the power to incite action *"Will the Lord cast off for ever? and will he be favorable no more? Is his mercy clean gone forever? doth his promise fail for evermore? Hath God forgotten to be gracious? hath he in anger shut up his tender mercies? Selah. And I said, This is my infirmity: but I will remember the years of the right hand of the most High. I will remember the works of the Lord: surely I will remember thy wonders of old"* Psalm 77:7-11. Remembering is essentially looking back, and it most certainly, at least in this case, is intended to compare the present with the past. It is a most helpful means for discovering where we are, and of awakening us to our present condition. So let us with all honesty seek to remember. Let us not wait until drastic measures are employed for turning us around. *"When he slew them, then they sought him: and they returned and inquired early after God. And they remembered that God was their rock, and the high God their redeemer"* Psalm 78:34,35.

Having remembered and evaluated our present status, and having discovered our deficiency and loss, the next and most vital step is repentance. To repent is to begin to think with God. We tend to forget that, as God states it, *"For my thoughts are not your thoughts, neither are your ways my ways"* Isaiah 55:8. And because of forgetting we must, by a deliberate act, remember.

Remembering is intended to provoke us to repentance, to turn us away from our own destructive thinking to His thinking. Hear it well! *"Let the wicked forsake his way, and the unrighteous man **his thoughts**; and let him return unto the Lord, and he will have mercy upon him; and to our God, for he will abundantly pardon"* (55:7).

Repentance guarantees reparation. Only that kind of repentance described in the passage above has the power to restore and reestablish that "left" and lost first love. And only that can satisfy the heart of our deeply offended God. *"Turn us again, O God of hosts, and cause thy face to shine; and we shall be saved"* Psalm 80:7.

CHAPTER SIXTEEN

> "The teaching of sound doctrine is a prelude, if you will, to the supernatural. It is also a guide, a set of boundaries to keep emotions and exuberance within proper channels. In too many places where the Bible is being thumped and doctrine is being argued until three in the morning, the spirit of the doctrine is missing. William Law, an English devotional writer of the early 1700s wrote, 'Read whatever chapter you will, and be ever so delighted with it, yet it will leave you as poor, as empty and unchanged as it found you unless it has turned you wholly and solely to the Spirit of God, and brought you into full union with and dependence upon him.'"[19]
>
> Pastor Jim Cymbala

REPENTANCE AND DOCTRINAL ABERRATIONS

It is common knowledge that without a properly functioning heart, the human body deteriorates rapidly, finally ending in death. Similarly, the Church, devoid of sound doctrine or the victim of doctrinal aberrations, rapidly becomes spiritually anemic, and unless the condition is reversed, both spiritual declension and spiritual death are inevitable.

It is doubtful that there can be any more destructive force within the Church than false or aberrational doctrine. Doctrine is what we believe, and what we believe is what we will be. "You are what you eat!"

Our belief system controls us. If it is solidly and Biblically based, it can and does provide direction, assurance, hope, and much more. On the other hand, if it stands on the quick-sand of false doctrine, it will lead to certain and serious disaster.

Satan's most effective weapon against the Church is false doctrine. It brought to Adam and Eve ejection from God's garden, and robbed them of the glory with which they had been adorned. It yet remains that which has the potential for robbing the Church of all the glory that grace can provide. Thus doctrinal aberrations are a curse to the Church, and an object of utmost disdain to the Lord Himself.

Sound doctrine is imperative. Its absence creates a subtle vacuum, which in turn invites the intrusion of false doctrine. Truly, the lack of sound doctrine is the hot-bed for false doctrine.

It should not be overlooked that, in reality, our Lord was not addressing the Church at Pergamos directly, but rather His message was directed specifically to the angel of the church at Pergamos. That is of no little significance, for it places responsibility for conditions in that particular body squarely upon the shoulders of the Church's leadership. "Angel" can as well be translated "messenger." The implication is "pastor."

While, as is indicated, the Lord had "somewhat" against the Church at Ephesus, it is also indicated that He had a "few things" against the Church at Pergamos. With Ephesus the issue was "first love." With Pergamos it was "doctrine." While love is always the top priority consideration, doctrine holds a close second. Doctrinal aberration spells the sure disruption of Christian first love, just as untruthfulness and unfaithfulness are the sure underminers of human first love.

Yes, Pergamos had its problems. Indeed, serious problems. It appears that they were being countenanced and perhaps even discounted by the church's leadership rather than being confronted and handled. This displeased the Lord to such an extent that He required action or else.

An aside is in order at this point to underscore the grave responsibility of leadership. And not only leadership at the highest levels, but leadership at all levels. In the case of Pergamos, it was leadership at the local church level, the pastoral level.

In Israel's history is an account that should soundly alert all in leadership roles to their sacred charge. It is the sordid story of a high priest named Eli, and his two sons, Hophni and Phinehas. These were charged with Israel's spiritual leadership. Scripture says, *"Now the sons of Eli were sons of Belial; they knew not the Lord" 1 Samuel 2:12.* This is surely a case where nepotism overruled good judgment, and it brought tragedy and disaster in its wake.

Eli, being high priest, held the top-priority post in Israel's spiritual leadership. Yet he permitted his ungodly sons to remain in their leadership roles. In the face of their most despicable behavior he merely "slapped their wrists".

Read the account. *"And the priests' custom with the people was, that, when any man offered sacrifice, the priest's servant came, while the flesh was in seething, with a fleshhook of three teeth in his hand; And he struck it into the pan, or kettle, or caldron, or pot; all that the fleshhook brought up the priest took for himself. ' ...Also before they burnt the fat, the priest's servant came, and said to the man that sacrificed, Give flesh to roast for the priest; for he will not have sodden flesh of thee, but raw. And if any man said unto him, Let them not fail to burn the fat presently, and then take as much as thy soul desireth; then he would answer him, Nay; but thou shalt give it me now: and if not, I will take it by force. Wherefore the sin of the young men was very great before the Lord: for men abhorred the offering of the Lord"* 1 Samuel 2:13-17.

And note Eli's response: *"Now Eli was very old, and heard all that his sons did unto all Israel; and how they lay with the women that assembled at the door of the tabernacle of the congregation. And he said unto them, Why do ye such things? for I hear of your evil dealings by all this people. Nay, my sons; for it is no good report that I hear: ye make the Lord's people to transgress. If one man sin against another, the judge shall judge him: but if a man sin against the Lord, who shall intreat for him? Notwithstanding they hearkened not unto the voice of their father, because the Lord would slay them"* (2:22-25).

There was never any indication of remorse or repentance on the part of those two sons, nor is there an account showing Eli's honest attempt to correct the situation. All he did was to halfheartedly warn them. He certainly did not *"lay the axe unto the root."* So God did!

When spiritual leadership abdicates its assigned role, then God steps in. It is **repent** or else"! And all of Israel suffered God's "or else", for He permitted the Philistines to bitterly defeat them in battle. Eli's sons were both slain. The ark was taken, and Eli himself forfeited his life, whereupon his daughter-in-law, upon hearing the awful news, went into labor and bore a son whom she appropriately named, *"Ichabod, saying, The glory is departed from Israel"* 1 Samuel 4:21.

Now back to Pergamos. In the midst of her virtues, and she did have them (see *Revelation 2:13*), her pastor permitted or at least provided leeway for her doctrinal aberrations, in fact two of them, (1) the doctrine of Balaam and (2) the doctrine of the Nicolaitans.

What were these doctrines?

Let the scriptures themselves tell us. *"...thou hast there them that hold the doctrine of Balaam, who taught Balac to cast a stumblingblock before the children of Israel, to eat things sacrificed to idols, and to commit fornication" Revelation 2:14.* Again in *2 Peter 2:12-15*, Balaamism is described in rather shocking terms. *"But these, as natural brute beasts, made to be taken and destroyed, speak evil of the things that they understand not; and shall utterly perish in their own corruption; And shall receive the reward of unrighteouness as they that count it pleasure to riot in the day time. Spots they are and blemishes, sporting themselves with their own deceivings while they feast with you; Having eyes full of adultery, and that cannot cease from sin; beguiling unstable souls; an heart they have exercised with covetous practices; cursed children: Which have forsaken the right way, and are gone astray, following the way of Balaam the son of Bosor, who loved the wages of unrighteousness."*

Likely the key to best understanding the doctrine of Balaam is the final phrase of the passage above: *"who loved the wages of unrighteousness."* Balaamism taught what it did primarily for monetary advantage. Whatever it could say, whatever evil it could permit or advocate, whatever permissiveness it could allow, if it provided "cash-flow", that was its warrant. Never mind righteousness, lay aside principle, say or do whatever it takes to get into people's pockets or purses. Advocate immorality, or at least don't make an issue of it, condone idolatry, make license out of grace, whatever is necessary for gaining the desired end, do that.

What an insidious infection in the Church! What a force for undermining and destroying all that is good and right. And what a disgrace that it was permitted in the church!

But what of today? Are we, in any way confronted with aberrations similar to the doctrine of Balaam? Might we be blinded to Satan's devices? Remember, Pergamos was where "Satan's seat is" and "where Satan dwelleth". It is doubtful that that was more true of Pergamos than it might have been, or might be, of any other city. It was rather that Pergamos had given place to him. Give him place, and he will be seated. Howbeit, Paul counseled, *"Neither give place to the devil" Ephesians 4:27.*

In the Church, place is given to him whenever someone is granted room for fostering doctrinal aberration, as was the case in Pergamos.

A fearsome trend has risen in the Church today. It is the idea that doctrine is of little consequence. Doctrine, some believe, is a cold, dead subject. Doctrine, some think, doesn't really matter as long as one can prosper materially, feel good, be happy, worship energetically, perhaps dance in the aisles, shout loudly, and get all his earthly and physical desires and needs met.

The director of music, in a church of my acquaintance, announced at one point that the church really doesn't need the old hymns any longer. *"They are full of doctrine,"* he said, *"but what we need more is relationship."* However, the truth is, despite our admitted need for relationship, we never get beyond the need for doctrine. Relationship without doctrine tends to be like an automobile speeding down a freeway devoid of a steering wheel. Furthermore, sound doctrine leads to right relationships, both with God and with man.

Pastor Jim Cymbala, of the famed Brooklyn Tabernacle, said it well when he wrote, "The teaching of sound doctrine is a prelude, if you will, to the supernatural. It is also a guide, a set of boundaries to keep emotions and exuberance within proper channels" But he also sounded a warning, "In too many places where the Bible is being thumped and doctrine is being argued until three in the morning, the Spirit of the doctrine is missing. William Law, an English devotional writer of the early 1700s wrote, 'Read whatever chapter you will, and be ever so delighted with it, yet it will leave you as poor, as empty and unchanged as it found you, unless it has turned you wholly and solely to the Spirit of God, and brought you into full union with and dependence upon him' " 19

Now, because sound doctrine is depreciated, some are *"carried about with every wind of doctrine* (someone called it 'windy doctrine'), *by the slight of men, and cunning craftiness, whereby they lie in wait to deceive" Ephesians 4:14.*

I repeat, Wherever sound doctrine is lacking, there will be a floodtide of doctrinal aberrations to fill the void. Therefore, let us take heed.

While leadership is charged with planting and promoting sound doctrine, if it fails in that awesome assignment, it will sooner or later be confronted with doctrinal aberrations. The only way to successfully avoid doctrinal aberrations is to vigorously promote sound doctrine by every possible means.

Hence, it is of more consequence to promote sound doctrine than it is to purge doctrinal aberrations. Where sound doctrine abounds, doctrinal aberrations find little place for getting a foothold.

Fundamental to gaining sound doctrine is a heart for it. Jesus taught that *"If any man will do* (that is: willeth to do) *his will, he shall know of the doctrine, whether it be of God, or whether I speak of myself"*

John 7:17. The heart genuinely open for sound doctrine, and genuinely willing to conform to it, will have the distinct advantage of being able to recognize it for what it is. For the careless heart there will inevitably be doctrinal aberration. For the willing and committed heart there will be an understanding of the source of the doctrine. Encouraging indeed! Challenging for certain!

The Early Church was zealous for doctrine. It held a place of highest importance on its agenda. *"They continued **steadfastly** in the apostle's doctrine" Acts 2:42.* Evidently the Church at Pergamos had failed to do that. Thus the invasion or the intrusion of doctrinal aberration.

Again, the Early Church was committed to its doctrine. *"...and, behold, ye have filled Jerusalem with your doctrine" Acts 5:28.*

Paul was a zealot for sound doctrine. He recognized its vital role and he underscored its importance in his epistles. To Timothy he wrote, *"...that the mightiest charge some that they teach no other doctrine" 1 Timothy 1:3.* In the same chapter he warned of things *"contrary to sound doctrine" (vs. 10).*

Again and again doctrine was his emphasis. It holds a most significant place in his writings. *"If thou put the brethren in remembrance of these things, thou shalt be a good minister of Jesus Christ, nourished up in the words of faith and of good doctrine..." 1 Timothy 4:6. "Till I come, give attention to reading, to exhortation, to doctrine." (4:13). "Take heed unto thyself, and unto the doctrine; continue in them: for in doing this thou shalt both save thyself, and them that hear thee" (4:16). "Let the elders that rule well be counted worthy of double honor, especially they who labor in the word and doctrine" (5:17). "If any man teach otherwise, and consent not to wholesome words, even the words of our Lord Jesus Christ, and to the doctrine which is according to godliness" (6:3). "But thou hast fully known my doctrine, manner of life, purpose, faith, longsuffering, charity, patience" 2 Timothy 3:10. "All scripture is given by inspiration of God, and is profitable for doctrine, for reproof, for correction, for instruction in righteousness" (3:16). "Preach the word; be instant in season, out of season; reprove, rebuke, exhort with all longsuffering and doctrine. For the time will come when they will not endure sound doctrine; but after their own lusts shall they heap to themselves teachers, having itching ears" (4:2,3). "But speak thou the things which become sound doctrine" Titus 2:1. "In all things shewing thyself a pat-*

tern of good works: in doctrine shewing uncorruptness, gravity, sinceri-
ty" (2:7). "Not purloining, but shewing all good fidelity; that they may
adorn the doctrine of God our Saviour in all things" (2:10).

Pergamos had not heeded. Therefore she "came under the gun". Leadership had left the impression that sound doctrine was not of any particular import. And she had reaped a harvest. *"...thou hast there them (more than one) that hold the doctrine of Balaam."* That harvest brought or provoked the Lord's threat, "repent or else!"

Doctrinal aberration leads to more doctrinal aberration. From my farming days I recount that wild oats were a constant threat to our fields. If at any time we became lax or careless about eradicating them, they were sure to substantially hinder the wheat production, or even to virtually wipe it out. Eradication, though drastic, was the only sure solution to the problem.

And what of the doctrine of the Nicolaitans?

The doctrine of the Nicolaitans was very much like the doctrine of Balaam. All of the best manuscripts and versions support the idea that *Revelation 2:15* should begin, *"In like manner"* instead of *"So hast thou also"* as translated in the KJB, thus indicating the similarity of the two sects. Their doctrine was antinomian (that is the notion that under the gospel of grace, moral law is of no use or obligation, because faith alone is necessary to salvation), in principle, and licentious in result. They prostituted their influence by seducing God's people into impurity and idolatry.

While monetary gain was the overriding and corrupting factor in Balaamism, the gratification of sexual desire without restraint and the perversion of the true worship of God by idolatry was Nicolaitanism's cursed practice. In so doing they held that fornication and eating things offered to idols in honor of those idols were harmless practices.

"The sect flourishes still. Nicolaitans are everywhere, because everywhere there are men who will profess, believe, and do almost anything by which they think they may escape the hard necessity of obeying the moral laws of Christ. Well is it for the Church, well is it for everyone of us, to allow no pretense whatsoever to palliate evil deeds. Even the grace of God may be turned into lasciviousness, and it seems impossible to keep men back from presumptuous sins—sins, that is, for which they find, or think they find, encouragement in the doctrines of God's great mercy, and the all-atoning efficacy of our Saviour's death. But the Lord hates the deeds of such men, and may he help us to hate them too." [20]

Should we become aware of doctrinal aberrations in our belief system or in any part of the Church for which we have some responsibility, what then shall we do?

The answer is fixed. It never changes. It is forever the same. The requirement is, and was, and ever shall be "repent." After all, the offense in such matters first and foremost is against God. And repentance must be followed by adjustment and correction. Doctrinal aberration must be replaced by sound doctrine, and will demand diligent effort and application. It is more difficult to correct a doctrinal aberration once it has gained a foothold, than it is to avoid it in the first place.

The victim of doctrinal aberration, unless it is replaced with sound doctrine, is much like the man of whom Jesus spoke in *Luke 11:24-26*. *"When the unclean spirit is gone out of a man, he walketh through dry places, seeking rest; and finding none, he saith, I will return unto my house whence I cam out. And when he cometh, he findeth it swept and garnished. Then goeth he, and taketh to him seven other spirits more wicked than himself; and they enter in, and dwell there: and the last state of that man is worse than the first."*

Yes, in a sense, repentance sweeps and garnishes the house, but a house left empty is only an invitation to more false doctrine. The void must be filled. Therefore pursue sound doctrine.

A close look will show that much like the churches at Ephesus and Pergamous, Thyatira was also a victim of serious doctrinal error. We'll call their aberration Jezebelism, because the error was attributed directly to Jezebel. *"... thou sufferest that woman Jezebel, which calleth herself a prophetess, to teach and to seduce my servants to commit fornication, and to eat things sacrificed unto idols"* Revelation 2:20. Interestingly, one author suggests that the Jezebel identified was actually the wife of the pastor at Thyatira. Listen to what he says. *"Instead of that woman Jezebel...almost all ancient versions read...thy wife Jezebel; which intimates, indeed asserts, that this bad woman was the wife of the bishop of the church, and his criminality in suffering her was therefore the greater."* [21]

Whether "Jezebel", as employed in the text, was intended to indicate a real person, or whether the term was employed as a figure or a metaphor is much debated. If she was indeed the pastor's wife, then it appears he was doubly guilty. He was guilty of allowing her, in the first place, to promote her doctrinal aberrations of which he must have been aware. And, second, he was guilty of allowing her to continue her nefarious practice.

Doctrinal error, whatever form it may take in the hands of those who promote it, seems generally to run on the same track. At the heart of it is idolatry, and more often than not, it is idolatry of the first order. That is, the exaltation of one's self above God, and above His word. That was Jezebel! She called <u>herself</u> a prophetess, and she assumed the role of placing <u>her</u> doctrine above the doctrine of God. Strangely, too, she had a following as such people commonly do. Note, *"Behold, I will cast her..., **and them** that commit adultery with her into great tribulation" Revelation 2:22.* This does not necessarily infer physical adultery, but rather unfaithfulness to God Himself.

The prospect for any and all who follow such leadership is indeed bleak: *"Behold, I will kill her children (perhaps those who allied themselves with her) with death; and all the churches will know that I am he which searcheth the reins and hearts: and I will give to everyone of you according to your works" (2:23).*

Even so there is a ray of hope at the end of *verse 22: "except they repent." Let us therefore take heed to ourselves and unto our doctrine (see 1 Timothy 4:16).* It is no light matter. It is truly a life and death matter.

Repentance is required of both the perpetrator of the doctrinal aberration, and of the leadership which countenanced it. The perpetrator not only needs to grieve for having promoted it to the spiritual detriment of souls, but the leadership needs to grieve for having abdicated its assigned responsibility. And repentance in such cases must include more than sorrow for past action or inaction. It must demonstrate that repentance by a total about-face. The perpetrator must pursue sound doctrine, and the responsible leadership must see that he does it.

CHAPTER SEVENTEEN

> *Of the Laodicean church Matthew Henry wrote, "They were blind; they could not see their state, nor their way, nor their danger; they could not see into themselves; they could not look before them; they were blind and yet they thought they saw; the very light that was in them was darkness, and thus how great must that darkness be! They could not see Christ, though evidently set forth, and crucified before their eyes. They could not see God by faith, though always present in them. They could not see death, though it was just before them. They could not look into eternity though they stood on the very brink of it continually."* 23

REPENTANCE UNTO LIFE

God is at work! The central object of His activity is the Church. His goal is that *"we all come in the unity of the faith, and of the knowledge of the Son of God, unto a **perfect** man, unto the measure of the stature of the fulness of Christ" Ephesians 4:13* While seven individual churches are addressed in the Revelation, the obvious overriding concern is with **the Church.** The Church is the composite of all the churches, and each church is the composite of the people within itself. Therefore, when sin or error affects an individual in a church, that sin or error affects that particular church first and ultimately the whole Church.

The message to each of the seven churches is at once a measuring rod for that church, and the measuring rod for that church becomes a measuring rod for **the Church.** When an individual or a church fails to adhere to the "Blueprint," (the measure of the stature of the fulness of Christ), the Builder of the Church is displeased and disappointed.

Five of the seven churches of the Revelation were flawed. The flaw in the church at Ephesus was lost first love. In the church at Pergamos, it was doctrinal aberration; and in the church at Thyatira it was permissiveness, possibly the fruit of nepotism which allowed space for both doctrinal aberration and practice.

Now we come to Sardis. Her problem? *"...thou hast a name that thou livest, and art dead" Revelation 3:1.* What a sad commentary! What an indictment! Indeed, what a shocking revelation! Called alive, but dead!

The very possibility of being called alive while actually being dead is most frightening, to put it mildly. In the church at Sardis there were, as far as we know, no followers of Balaam, no Nicolaitans, and no followers of Jezebel. There appears to have been no inordinate pursuit of monetary gain, no indication of immorality or idolatry, no hint of tolerance toward false prophets or prophetesses, but there was death!

"This church had gained a great reputation; it had a name, and a very honorable one, for a flourishing church, a name for vital lively religion, for purity of doctrine, unity among themselves, uniformity in worship, decency, and order. We read not of any unhappy divisions among themselves. Everything appeared well, as to what falls under the observations of men.

"This church was not really what it was reputed to be. They had a name to live, but they were dead; there was a form of godliness, but not the power, a name to live, but not the principle of life. If there was not a total privation of life, yet there was a great deadness in their souls and in their services, a great deadness in the spirits of their ministers, and a great deadness in their ministrations, in their praying, in their preaching, in their converse, and a great deadness in the people hearing, in prayer, and in conversation; what little life was left among them was, in a manner, expiring, ready to die." [22]

What then was the real problem? It is of no little consequence that we discover it. What was at the heart of it? To find the answer in the case of the church at Sardis will be to become aware of a condition which might affect us, and which could also be as fatal for us as it was for them.

From my personal vantage point their problem was not a multiplicity of things. It was, in all likelihood, a single thing. However, no more serious thing could have happened to them or to any other church. Others of the seven churches had their problems, as we have already noted, but no other church had as grave a problem as that in the church at Sardis. What could be more fatal than death? What could be more final?

The Sardis church, from a purely human perspective, seemed to

have about everything going for it, the topmost being "a name that thou
livest." It had reputation. It had works. But it lacked the one thing that
could make all else meaningful from an eternal perspective. Tragically,
and beyond everything else, it evidently lacked the one Person whom the
church was all about. It lacked the Lord, Jesus Himself! It lacked the
Lifegiver! It lacked Him who had said, *"I am the resurrection and **the
life"** John 11:25.* It lacked Him who had said, *"I am the way, the truth,
and **the life"** (14:6).* Does not scripture tell us, *"When Christ who is **our
life** shall appear, then shall ye also appear with him in glory"?
Colossians 3:4.* And we must also recall John's word, *"He that hath the
Son **hath life;** and he that hath not the Son of God **hath not life"** 1 John
5:12.* It is as simple as that. Have the Son, have life. Have everything
else but the Son, have death instead of life.

Have a name. Have a reputation. Have a crowd. Have beautiful
singing. Have capable preaching. Have excitement. Have a form of worship. Have good organization. Have fine facilities. Have financial
strength. Have a program of activity. Have everything you can think of;
yet, in the face of all of that, if the Son is absent, so also is the life absent,
and so death is present.

Much activity and much resources do not guarantee the presence
of spiritual life. One can sing loudly and lustily; one can preach like a
prophet. One can perform profoundly, and yet be devoid of vital relationship with Christ. Our Lord Himself said it ever so plainly, *"Many will
say to me in that day, Lord, Lord, have we not prophesied in thy name?
and in thy name have cast out devils? and in thy name done many won-
derful works? And then will I profess unto them, I never knew you:
depart from me, ye that work iniquity" Matthew 7:22,23.*

Sardis had had Him and His life. Now they had lost Him and His
life. They were like Samson of old. At a point in his life the Spirit of God
wrought mightily through Him. He had "life." Whenever the Spirit of the
Lord came upon him, he did tremendous exploits. He slew a lion with his
bare hands, he slew a thousand Philistines with the jawbone of an ass, he
carried away the gates of Gaza to the top of a hill near Hebron on his
shoulders. He did marvelously. But he lived carelessly. He consorted with
ungodly women. He violated moral law. In a sense we can say he died,
for *"he wist not that the Lord was departed from him" Judges 16:20.* He
had a name and a reputation that he was "alive", but he was "dead"!

Israel's King Saul was little different. He began well. Samuel had told him, *"...the Spirit of the Lord will come upon thee, and thou shalt prophesy with them, and shalt be turned into another man"* 1 Samuel 10:6. *"And it was so, that when he had turned his back to go from Samuel, God gave him another heart"* (10:9). Indeed he was "alive". and for a period of time he demonstrated that life in his leadership role. He was humble and dependent. He was timid and retiring. But soon he became proud and self-serving, and he gave himself over to another spirit. He disobeyed God's clear directives, eventually determining to slay David whom God had chosen to succeed him, and it was said of him *"for he is such a son of Belial, that a man cannot speak to him"* (25:17).

Hear his fearful end: *"Then said Samuel, Wherefore then dost thou ask of me, seeing the Lord is departed from thee, and is become thine enemy? And the Lord hath done to him as he spake by me: for the Lord hath rent the kingdom out of thine hand, and given it to thy neighbour even to David: because thou obeyest not the voice of the Lord, nor executedest his fierce wrath upon Amalek, therefore hath the Lord done this thing unto thee this day"* 1 Samuel 28:16-18.

"And the battle went sore against Saul, and the archers hit him; and he was sore wounded of the archer. Then said Saul unto his armourbearer, Draw thy sword, and thrust me through therewith; lest these uncircumcised come and thrust me through, and abuse me. But his armourbearer would not; for he was sore afraid. Therefore Saul took a sword, and fell upon it" (31:3-4).

Once he had prophesied with the prophets. Once he was very much alive unto God. But, sadly, all of that had changed, and now he was dead! Dead! Dead!

Is there any chance that Sardis might bespeak a condition in a segment of the Church today? Is there the possibility that that segment might have a name, a reputation that it is alive, and yet, it is actually dead? Certainly a worrisome possibility.

There is an interesting line in Ecclesiastes that states ... *"the dead know not anything"* (vs. 9:5). The reference is obviously to the physically dead, but since the physical illustrates the spiritual, it can be safely concluded that one can be dead spiritually, and yet be totally oblivious of the condition. The frightening truth is, the dead are unaware of their own deadness.

So the question must be asked, How can I as an individual know whether or not I am spiritually alive? And, likewise, how can a church know? Another question should also be posed: How does spiritual life bear witness of itself? So very much hinges on sound answers to these questions.

In the outset, it should be understood that inquiry and concern are themselves indicators of life. Assuredly, where there is no inquiry and no concern, that in itself portends death. One of the positive indications of physical life is the simple act of eating and drinking. When there is no eating and no drinking, either death has already occurred or it is imminent.

Some years ago the Rev. J. D. Kesler, who was my first pastor, was in the hospital. I went to visit him and he told me that he no longer had any desire to eat. In a few days I preached his funeral.

It is no different spiritually. When hunger for the living Bread, Jesus Himself, and thirst for the living water, the Word of God, are no longer present, and when there is no heart-cry for fellowship and communion with the Father and the Son, these are omens of pending death, or even of death itself.

How, then, may an individual soul or a church discover its true state? Perhaps by confronting honestly a series of questions. It is likely the answers will speak for themselves.

1. Do I hunger for God's Word, and do I make it my daily diet?
   'And he humbled thee, and suffered thee to hunger, and fed thee with manna, which thou knewest not, neither did thy fathers know; that he might make thee know that man doth not live by bread only, but by every word that proceedeth out of the mouth of the Lord doth man live" Deuteronomy 8:3.
2. Do I thirst for God, and for the knowledge of Him?
   "My soul thirsteth for God, for the living God: when shall I come and appear before God?" Psalm 42:2.
3. Does any awareness of sin in my life cause me to cry for mercy and forgiveness?
4. Is sin, to me, as sinful as it once was?
5. Do I find myself troubled at the lusts of the flesh?
6. Do I strive to "die daily" to my sinful nature?
7. Is pleasing God a top-priority concern of mine?
8. Has my love of things and pleasure replaced my love for God?
9. Is personal prayer my daily practice?
10. Is attendance at God's house an important part of my lifestyle?

And what are some questions a church should ask of itself?

1. Is Christ and His cross preached?
2. Is the church truly a house of prayer?
3. Is prayer in the church anything more than a perfunctory performance?
4. Is the Holy Spirit recognized and honored and revered in the church?
5. Is there room for the supernatural in the service?
6. Do we exult in God's manifested presence in the services?
7. Is the church's membership requirement based upon Biblical standards of godly conduct?

Quite obviously more questions could be asked, but those already asked should give us a sense of direction. Any "no" answer is symptomatic of death. "Yes" answers indicate life.

In Sardis the "no" answers must have been in preponderance. Therefore they had *"a name that thou livest, and art dead."*

What, then, is the answer to such lifelessness?—to such death? Jesus gave it. *"Remember therefore how thou hast received and heard, and hold fast, and repent. If therefore thou shalt not watch, I will come on thee as a thief, and thou shalt not know what hour I will come upon thee"* Revelation 3:3.

Repentance was the only answer for Sardis. Repentance is the only answer for us. Repentance would revive Sardis. Repentance will revive us. Remember, *"Then hath God also to the Gentiles granted repentance **unto life**"* Acts 11:18. He will also grant us repentance <u>unto life</u> for our spiritual deadness. <u>Repent therefore!</u>

Then there was the church at Laodicea, the last and, in some sense, the worst of the seven churches named in the Revelation. While the church at Philadelphia received no reproval from her Lord, this church received no commendation. We in the church today ought to take serious note, lest we awaken to discover that we have more in common with Laodicea than with Philadelphia.

The Laodicean church, planted perhaps by none less than the Apostle Paul himself, was situated in a famous and prosperous city near the river Lycus in Phrygia. The city's wealth was demonstrated when, upon being destroyed by an earthquake, it was rebuilt without outside financial assistance.

Let's endeavor to discover what it was about this particular church that drew such severe denunciation. Jesus Himself warned them of their condition. He said, *"You are neither cold nor hot. You are luke-*

warm, and therefore I will spew you out of my mouth."

I identify with His disappointment, for I like my coffee barely less than boiling, and my drinking water just above freezing.

The Laodicean lukewarmness, evidently born out of self-deception, was the issue. No one is more deceived than the self-deceived. The Laodiceans said, *"We are rich."* Jesus said, *"You are poor."* They said, *"We are increased with goods."* He said, *"You are wretched and miserable."* They said, *"We have need of nothing."* He said, *"You are blind and naked."*

What a contrast between perception and fact!

They perceived themselves to be rich. Whether they were thinking of their spiritual condition or their financial state, or even of both, is not clear. In any case their thinking was flawed. What can be more serious than misjudging one's own spiritual state? And what also is more dangerous than fancying one's self to be what he is not? — a dwarf fancying himself a giant, a pauper thinking himself a millionaire, a beggar perceiving of himself to be a king. But in no way can Jesus countenance such fancying when spiritual reality is involved. Nor do His children dare allow themselves the "luxury" of such deception. Too much is at stake.

The Laodicean deception manifested itself in their mistaken idea that they had it "made in the shade" spiritually, while in reality their condition was so wretched that Jesus was about to spew them out of His mouth.

In their own eyes they were rich. Indeed they had been benefactors of God's great grace. No doubt it had delivered them from their previous paganism. It had given them new life and had eventuated in their forming the church of which they were now a part. Were they on the scene today we might hear them singing John Newton's *"Amazing grace, how sweet the sound, that saved a wretch like me. I once was lost, but now I'm found, was blind, but now I see."*

They testified, *"We are increased with goods."* Not only had they been enlightened by the gospel and cleansed from their sin by the blood of the Lamb, but in all likelihood they had been baptized in the Holy Spirit. They were charismatic. No doubt they had witnessed and experienced the supernatural, and had seen the gifts of the Spirit operate in their own lives, and in their church.

Hence, they had concluded, *"We have need of nothing."* Let it be noted here that a need unrecognized is as serious a problem as is the need itself. Until need is recognized and admitted, solution to a problem will not be sought. Jesus said, *"They that be whole need not a physician, but* *they that are sick . But go ye and learn what that meaneth, I will have mercy, and not sacrifice; for I am not come to call the righteous but sinners **to repentance**" Matthew 9:12, 13.*

Jesus' whole point in His letter to the church of Laodicea was to awaken them to their condition, and thus to provoke them to repentance. No, ignorance is not bliss, and 'tis not folly to be wise. It is Satan who seeks to disguise reality, and to foster and promote ignorance. But, God who is light, ever seeks to bring men to reality, to dispel darkness, and to replace ignorance with knowledge.

Therefore, Jesus said to the Laodiceans, *"thou art wretched and miserable."* The identical word *wretched* is found in *Romans 8:24* wherein Paul speaks of a condition in which he found himself, *"O wretched man that I am!"* And the NEB translates the Revelation statement regarding Laodicea, *"the most pitiful wretch."* What a wake-up call!

And Jesus continued His exposure of the church by saying, *"thou art...poor"*. They thought they were rich. He said they were the exact opposite, they were poor. How could that be? Hadn't they experienced the riches of His grace? Hadn't they experienced *"the mystery of God, and of the Father, and of Christ; in whom are hid all the treasures of wisdom and knowledge"? Colossians 2:2,3.* How could it be that while they reveled in their riches, He was revolted by their poverty?

Likely the erosion was a process. It didn't happen in a day. The Bible speaks of the deceitfulness of riches. Could it be that the material wealth of Laodicea had slowly but surely gnawed away at the true riches until it had replaced them and that they had failed to recognize the folly of their own ways? *"The first and worst of all frauds,"* say Festus, *"is to cheat one's self."*

And what of us? Are we discerning the difference between the true riches and those riches which take wings and fly away? Are we in the same boat with the Laodiceans? Have we become deprived of the true riches by the riches of an affluent society? What kind of prosperity has priority in our thinking? Is material wealth our criteria for judging spiritual prosperity? Do we remember that covetousness is idolatry? Have we noted the contrast between the church at Smyrna and the church at Laodicea? To Smyrna Jesus said, *"I know thy ...poverty, but thou art rich" Revelation 2:9.* To Laodicea He said, *"thou sayest I am rich...but thou art...poor" (3:17).* Are we remembering Paul's counsel to Timothy, *"But they that will be rich fall into temptation and a snare, and into many foolish and hurtful lusts, which drown men in destruction and perdition?"*

1 Timothy 6:9.

Do we pay any attention to James' woe-filled warning? *"Go to now, ye rich men, weep and howl for your miseries that shall come upon you. Your riches are corrupted, and your garments are motheaten. Your gold and silver is cankered; and the rust of them shall be a witness against you, and shall eat your flesh as it were fire. Ye have heaped treasure together for the last days... Ye have lived in pleasure on the earth and been wanton; ye have nourished your hearts, as in a day of slaughter"* James 5:1-3,5.

It seems quite evident that the Laodicean church had fallen victim to its own material prosperity, and that its glitter had blinded their eyes to the true riches.

Now, not only were they, by the Lord's appraisal, wretched and miserable, and poor. They were blind, blind to their present condition and to their true spiritual state. They had become blind to the spiritual reality and experience they once knew, and blind to the eternal consequences should their present condition prevail.

Of them Matthew Henry says, "They were blind; they could not see their state, nor their way, nor their danger; they could not see into themselves; they could not look before them; they were blind, and yet they thought they saw; the very light that was in them was darkness, and then how great must that darkness be! They could not see Christ, though evidently set forth, and crucified before them. They could not look into eternity, though they stood on the very brink of it continually." [23]

Physical blindness is a most severe handicap, but it doesn't hold a candle to that blindness of the soul. The physically blind are extremely aware of their condition, but Jesus said of the Laodiceans, *"and knowest not that thou are...blind."*

Is it possible that we in His Church at the turn of the century have gone blind? Do we see as once we saw? Or might we be counted with the Laodiceans? Lord, help us see ourselves as you see us! Open our eyes before it is too late.

One more word. They were naked. To be naked is to be unclothed. Once they had been clothed upon with the garments of His righteousness. Now, they were unclothed! Can one thus clothed upon be unclothed? Evidently the Laodiceans didn't think so. Yet Jesus said so. *"You are...naked!"* What an extreme condition is nakedness! The naked cannot survive for long.

As these lines are being written, one of Texas' most notorious prisoners has escaped despite almost insurmountable odds. From the highest security area of the prison, over wall after wall and fence after fence, even fences bedecked with razor blade sharp obstacles, he managed to gain his freedom. And as he fled into a forested area beyond the prison, in order to elude his would-be captors, he totally removed all of his garments. He is naked. But it is certain that unless he is captured and taken back into custody he will likely die post haste, for the area wherein he is hiding is infested with poisonous snakes and mosquitoes.

Spiritual nakedness is even more disastrous. To stand naked before God's judgment throne is not a pleasant prospect. What worse thing could happen to a person, especially to one who was once clothed with the garments of Christ's righteousness?

Listen carefully to the message in the following verses by: S. Conway.

"In the silent midnight watch,
List! thy bosom door!
How it knocketh—knocketh—knocketh—
Knocketh evermore!
Say not 'Tis thy pulse is beating:
'Tis thy heart of sin;
'Tis thy Saviour knocks and crieth,
'Rise and let me in.'

"Death comes on with reckless footsteps,
To the hall and hut,
Think you, Death will tarry knocking
Where the door is shut?
Jesus waiteth—waiteth—waiteth,
But the door is fast;
Grieved, away thy Saviour goeth:
Death breaks in at last.

"Then 'tis time to stand entreating
Christ to let thee in;
At the gate of heaven beating,
Waiting for thy sin.
Nay, alas! thou guilty creature;
Hast thou then forgot?

> *Jesus waited long to know thee,*
> *Now he knows thee not."*
>   *—S.C.* [24]

Lest the piercing and penetrating message of those verses become reality for anyone reading these lines, or for anyone else to whom Jesus conveys the Laodicean message, let it be known that such evil consequences are avoidable.

Here is how: *"...be zealous therefore, and repent"* Revelation 3:19.

1. *"...buy of me gold tried in the fire, that thou mayest be rich,"*
2. *"...buy of me...white raiment, that thou mayest be clothed, and that the shame of they nakedness do not appear,"*
3. *"...anoint thine eyes with eyesalve; that thou mayest see"* (3:18).

Is Jesus knocking at your door?

CHAPTER EIGHTEEN

> *Turning from the way man thinks of sin, to the way God thinks of sin, and then acting accordingly—that is likely the ultimate definition of repentance.*

REPENTANCE: THINKING WITH GOD

Man's mind is the control tower of his soul. His act is the thought of his mind expressed. His sinful acts are the fruit of his sinful thoughts. From Adam's day to ours, man's behavior patterns have followed close on the heels of his thought patterns. The wise Solomon observed, *"For as he thinketh in his heart, so is he" Proverbs 23:7.*

Man's mind and its thought processes are his most monumental problem. Paul states that the carnal (human) mind is enmity against God (*Romans 8:7*). And Jeremiah agrees when he says, *"The heart* (mind) *is deceitful above all things, and desperately wicked: who can know it?" John 17:9.* Even before the great flood, *"God saw that the wickedness of man was great in the earth, and that every imagination of the **thoughts of his heart** was only evil continually" Genesis 6:5.* God's thinking about sin, and man's thinking about sin tend to be far apart. God says, *"For my thoughts are not your thoughts, neither are your ways my ways... For as the heavens are higher than the earth, so are my ways higher than your ways, and my thoughts than your thoughts" Isaiah 55:8,9.*

So what are God's thoughts about sin? Certainly He thinks differently than we do. His Word and His acts tell us in no uncertain terms. His Word is His thought verbalized. His acts are His thoughts demonstrated. By His Word we acquire the knowledge of sin. By His acts we understand His thoughts and His view of sin.

In like manner, what man thinks of sin is evidenced by his acts. Before every sinful act is a sinful thought. *"But every man is tempted, when he is drawn away of his own lust and enticed" James 1:14.* To lust, and to be enticed, is to think upon the pleasure, the gratification, and the satisfaction to be derived from a sinful act. It is to think opposite to what God thinks of the sinfulness of the act and likewise of the certainty of its consequence. Man's thinking of sin then becomes the seed planted which, in turn, produces the sinful act which follows. *Then when lust hath conceived, it bringeth forth sin; and sin when it is finished* (that is: when it is consummated) *bringeth forth death" James 1:15.* Thus the order of events in God's mind is: 1) thought, 2) act, and 3) death. *"The soul that sinneth, it shall die" Ezekiel 18:20.*

Jesus drew the line even more tightly. His word is, "Y*e have heard that it was said of them of old time, Thou shalt not commit adultery: But I say unto you, That whosoever looketh upon a woman to lust after her* (that is to think of the fleshly pleasure a sexual relationship with her would give him) *hath committed adultery with her already in his heart" Matthew 5:28.* Thus man thinks of adultery as a pleasure, and he chooses the pleasure of that sin above accepting and being guided by what God thinks of that sin.

Remember, He has told us that His thoughts are higher than our thoughts. What does God think of adultery? He has stated exactly what He thinks: *"And the man that committeth adultery with another man's wife, even he that committeth adultery with his neighbor's wife, the adulterer and the adultress shall be put to death" Leviticus 20:10.*

Man thinks of the pleasure. God thinks of the fruit of that pleasure. Man thinks in relation to time. God thinks in relation to eternity. In both instances the thought is followed by the act. In the case of man, the thought of adultery is followed by the act of adultery. In the case of God, His thought relating to man's thought and subsequent act are followed by His inposing the death penalty, which is required by His absolute justice.

What is true of adultery is true of all sin. In the mind of God, sin is sin, and all sin must suffer its own consequence.

At this very moment the cup of iniquity in our land is fast filling up. While man's sinning grows more obvious and bold and intense, judgment looms ominously on the horizon. Therefore we urgently need to call to remembrance the account of two cities cited repeatedly in Scripture for an effective demonstration and example of the difference between man's thoughts and God's thoughts. They are Sodom and Gomorrah. We can learn from them.

Sin reigned in them. It was flagrant, and open, and violent. It increased in intensity and kind, until it found its most extreme expression in the most deviant forms of sexuality—homosexuality and lesbianism.

In *Romans 1:24-27*, Paul states the rationale and the evolution (if I may employ that term) of such behavior: *"...because they exchanged the truth about God for a lie and worshipped and served the creature rather than the Creator, who is blessed forever! Amen. For this reason God gave them up to degrading passions. Their women exchanged natural intercourse for unnatural, and in the same way also the men, giving up natural intercourse with women, were consumed with passion for one another. Men committed shameful acts with men and received in their own persons the due penalty for their error"* (The New RSV).

Furthermore, *Genesis 13:13* speaks to the conditions in Sodom. *"But the men of Sodom were wicked sinners before the Lord exceedingly."*

"In ancient Sodom, homosexuals came out of their closets and became activists, casting a demonic spell over an entire generation of men and boys. They grew politically powerful, controlling everything. And Sodom became the world's gay capitol—a society so vile, wicked and crazed with violence that its sins thundered throughout the heavens, filling God's holy environment with a hellish cry.

"God dispatched two angels to Sodom, and it seemed even they were shocked by the utter degradation and wickedness they saw. This society mocked family values. (How could any society ruled by a militant homosexual spirit not witness the destruction of decent family life?) No visiting male was safe in Sodom. Roving gangs of homosexuals freely cruised the streets and alleys, looking for rape victims. And no one dared stop them—no politician, no police officer, no uprising of enraged parents." [25]

Yes, even angels were not safe in Sodom, for they became the target of the ferocious, debauched, and lust-crazed appetite of the Sodomites, whose evident only thought was their debased fleshly desire. Look at the account: *"And there came two angels to Sodom at even; and Lot sat in the gate of Sodom: and Lot seeing them rose up to meet them; and he bowed himself with his face toward the ground; And he said, Behold now, my lords, turn in, I pray you, into your servant's house, and tarry all night, and wash your feet, and ye shall rise up early, and go on your ways. And they said, Nay; but we will abide in the street all night. And he pressed upon them greatly; and they turned in unto him, and entered into his house; and he made them a feast, and did bake unleavened bread, and they did eat. But before they lay down, the men of the city, even the men of Sodom, compassed the house round, both old and young, all the people from every quarter: And they called unto Lot, and said unto him, Where are the men which came in to thee this night? bring them out unto us, that we may know them"* Genesis 19:1-5.

What had been true of men in Noah's day was true of Sodom, and it is fast becoming true in America. *"Every imagination of the **thoughts** of his heart was only evil continually"* (Genesis 6:5). God was not in their thoughts, but they were in God's thoughts.

Homosexuality is dangerously on the rise in America. Gays are no longer confined to their closets. They are in prominent places. They unashamedly demand their rights. They play significant roles in politics (being recognized and promoted by none less than our former U. S. president and vice president). They serve as pastors, and are fast gaining denominational recognition. They parade their cause boldly, defying God at every turn of the way.

But what does God think? He thinks as He has always thought. He has not changed His mind. His thoughts are plainly stated so that none need miss them. *"And turning the cities of Sodom and Gomorrha into ashes; condemned them with an overthrow, making them an ensample unto those that after would live ungodly"* 2 Peter 2:6.

If you really want to know what God thinks of sin, not only of the sin of homosexuality (that being sin near its most extreme degree) but of all sin, and in whatever form it may appear, don't relay merely on your own thoughts, nor on the thoughts of philosophers, nor on the thoughts of psychological counselors, nor on the thoughts of non-evangelical religionists, nor on the thoughts of politicians, nor yet on the thoughts of men in general But look instead to God's thoughts and acts as they relate to sin. Above all, look to Gethsemane and to Calvary. Look to the garden and to the cross. There is the most profound revelation of God's thoughts and acts regarding sin that the world has ever witnessed.

Listen to the anguished cry of none less than the Son of God, Himself, on that darkest of nights in Gethsemane. *"My soul is exceeding sorrowful, even unto death"* Mark 14:34, and hear His painfilled plea, *"Abba, father, all things are possible unto thee; take away this cup from me"* (14:36). Therein is revealed the thought of God about the sin of man. Those thoughts nearly slew Jesus before ever He got to the cross. Those thoughts had to do with His taking the fearful death-dealing sin of man upon Himself. That cup which Jesus faced was so fearful, so frightening, so terror-ridden that He repeatedly pled that it might be removed, that He might avoid drinking it.

Some have thought that that cup was a representation of Jesus' impending death on the cross, and certainly who wouldn't disdain such a prospect? But I am persuaded it represented more than that. Yes, far more than that. It is my personal persuasion and view that that cup represented the whole unbearable load of man's sins, and that that was the reason for Jesus' extreme and anguished repulsion. U.S. Grant, a very able preacher of yesteryear, stated it so well when he wrote, *"We can only conjecture, but the strong inference is that it was the cup of iniquity in which were the sins of the whole world. All the horrible sins of mankind (and some believe our diseases, too) were in that cup. His sinless character is what made that cup so repulsive."* His reaction revealed in unparalleled fashion what God thinks of sin.

So what does man think of that cup of iniquity and what does God think of it? Man thinks of it as a cup from which to drink. God thinks of it as a cup to be despised and avoided, if at all possible. Man thinks of it as a scource of excitement, fleshly gratification and pleasure. God thinks of it as the mainspring of deepest agony and unbearable sorrow. Man thinks of it as something to be desired, and even to be pursued. God thinks of it as something to flee at all cost, and to be mightily disdained. Man thinks of the cup in the light of the present, the now. God thinks of it in the light of the future, the "then." Man sees it with "blinded" eyes. God views it with eyes wide open.

Hear me now! Hear me now! God has drawn the curtain, and He has placed on center-stage the most awesome revelation of His thinking about sin the whole universe has ever witnessed. The setting was the Garden of Gethsemane and the cross on Mount Calvary. The main "actor" was His own Son, the Lord Jesus. What happened there was not a mere act. It was the actual playing out of reality, and the most profound revelation of sin's monstrous destructive force and consequence.

To fathom Jesus' incomprehensible horror there is to penetrate the realm of God's thinking about sin. Yes, of any and of all sin. Surely, Gethsemane was not merely the incomparable battlefield of the ages, it was also the most profound demonstration of God's thinking relative to sin and evil known to man. Combine Gethsemane with Calvary and you no longer need to wonder how God views sin, and what He thinks of it.

In Gethsemane Jesus faced the most demanding, the darkest, and most desperate moment in both time and eternity There had never been an hour like this one. You can sense His utter despair in His cry, *"Now is my soul troubled: and what shall I say? Father, save me from this hour, but for this cause came I unto this hour"* John 12:27. To drink the cup was to forfeit His equality with God, and His being, *"holy, harmless, undefiled, separate from sinners"* Hebrews 7:26. It was to join the ranks of the sinful. Isaiah tells us, *"...he was numbered* (inventoried) *with the transgressors, and he bear the sins of many" (53:12).* And Paul explains, *"He hath made him to be sin for us, who knew no sin"* 2 Corinthians 5:21.

The struggle was, in no sense of the word, an easy one. The pressure was so intense it forced the blood from His veins so that *"his sweat was as it were great drops of blood falling down to the ground"* Luke 22:44. But in the end He won. He did the will of the Father. He drank from the cup! He became sin for us! O glorious truth!

And from thence He went to Calvary. He went bearing the sin of all men everywhere, from Adam in Eden to the last man on earth, wherever and whoever he may be. He admitted to guilt for all men's sins when, as Isaiah states it, *"he is brought as a lamb to the slaughter, and as a sheep before her shearers is dumb, so he openeth not his mouth" (53:7).* His silence was his admission of guilt, not for any sin of His own, but for all men's sins, by substitution.

Guilt, whether for sins committed, or guilt for sins assumed, requires the death penalty. God can make no exceptions. Wherever and whenever there is guilt, there will also be death. *"In the day that thou eatest thereof thou shalt die"* Genesis 2:15. (Perhaps better translated "dying thou shalt die.") *"The soul that sinneth, it shall die"* Ezekiel 18:4. *"For the wages of sin is death"* Romans 6:23.

But Jesus, having assumed full responsibility and guilt for man's sin, bore that sin to the cross, and *"after he had offered one sacrifice for sins forever, sat down on the right hand of God"* Hebrews 10:12. He paid the ultimate penalty in full, *"for in that he died, he died unto sin once* (that is: he died unto sin once for all; for all sin, for all men, for all time): *but in that he liveth, he liveth unto God"* Romans 6:10. Therefore we have the highest incentive to shout Hallelujah!

Why would Jesus elect thus to die? For good reason: *"who for the joy that was set before him, endured the cross, despising the shame, and is set down at the right hand of the throne of God"* Hebrews 12:2. *"He shall see the travail of his soul, and shall be satisfied"* Isaiah 53:11.

That then brings all men face to face with reality. Will we permit Him to have suffered so fiercely, and to have died so ignominiously, for us in vain? Every man must decide for himself. Will he go on thinking his own thoughts, walking in his own ways, and acting accordingly, or will he rather seek to satisfy that One who is forever waiting and watching for his positive response?

Opportunity is fast fading. Conditions worsen daily.

"What ails our American Society? How can a whole nation party, dance, drink and be saturated with entertainment, while thousands of babies are being aborted? What kind of disease has so blinded our nation that the President could veto a bill outlawing doctors from sucking out the brains of babies just weeks before they're born? What horrible sickness allows our society to continue merrily in its sordid pleasure-seeking, while the elderly are being assisted in suicide? America is under siege by an army of abortionists, pornographers, drug pushers, murderers of the elderly, coming at us from all corners of the earth. And yet, only a few prophetic voices can be heard!" [26]

America is not unlike Israel to whom the prophet spoke long ago: *"...for the Lord hath a controversy with the inhabitants of the land, because there is no truth, nor mercy, nor knowledge of God in the land. By swearing, and lying, and killing, and stealing, and committing adultery, they break out, and blood toucheth blood. Therefore shall the land mourn, and everyone that dwelleth therein shall languish, with the beasts of the field, and with the fowls of heaven; and the fishes of the sea also shall be taken away...My people are destroyed for lack of knowledge: because thou hast rejected knowledge, I will also reject thee...seeing thou hast forgotten the law of thy God, I will also forget thy children. As they were increased, so they sinned against me: therefore will I change their glory into shame. They eat up the sin of my people, and they set their heart on their iniquity...and I will punish them for their ways, and reward them their doings. For they shall eat, and not have enough: they shall commit whoredom, and shall not increase: because they have left off to take heed to the Lord. Whoredom and wine and new wine take away the heart"* Hosea 4:1-4,6-11.

What then shall we do to avert such impending calamity and certain disaster? Is it already too late, or is there yet hope? Where there is life, there is hope; and we might add, while there is time, there is opportunity. So let us heed His word: *"Seek ye the Lord **while he may be*** *found*, call upon him **while he is near.** *Let the wicked forsake his way, and the unrighteous man his thoughts: and let him return unto the Lord, and he will have mercy upon him, and to our God, for he will abundantly pardon" Isaiah 55:6-7.* A single word says it all. REPENT, turn away from thinking of sin as men think of it, and turn to thinking of sin the way God thinks of it. And then act accordingly.

All of God's blessings follow close on the heels of repentance. Repentance is the white horse that lead the parade. Repentance is the rainbow, signaling the storm's end. It is the oasis in the desert for the weary traveler. Only repentance can lead men back to God. It must begin with the Church, with us, with you and with me. It is indeed *"The axe...laid unto the root!"* It is the cry of the Spirit today!

BIBLIOGRAPHY

1. *The Pulpit Commentary on 2 Peter*, pages 28 and 40; published by Hendrickson Publisher Peabody, Massachusetts 01969-3473

2. *Theological Dictionary of the New Testament*, by Geoffry W. Bromily, pages 640-641 published by William B. Eerdmans Pub. Co., 255 Jefferson Ave. SE, Grand Rapids, MI 40503

3. Ibid., pages 642-643

4. Ibid., page 643

5. *Judgment and Mercy*, by F. W. Farrar, page 170; published by E. P. Dutton and Company, 713 Broadway, New York, NY.

6. *The Pulpit Commentary on 1 Samuel*, page 268; published by Hendrickson Publishers, Peabody, Massachusetts 01961-3473

7. Matthew Henry's *Commentary*, Vol. 1, page 532; Published by Hendrickson Publishers, Peabody, Massachusetts 01961-3473

8. *The Pulpit Commentary*, Vol. 14, page 274

9. Ibid., Vol. 21, page 359

10. *Pathway to Peace*, by R. D. Ross (devotional for October 30); published by Scott Pub. Co., Kalispell MT. (Used by permission.)

11. *The Pulpit Commentary on Joel*, Vol. 13, Introduction to Joel pages iii and iv.

12. Adam Clarke's *Commentary*, Vol. 4, pages 630-631. Published by Abington-Cokesbury Press, New York-Nashville.

13. Matthew Henry's *Commentary*, Vol. 4, page 853.

14. Author unknown.

15. *The Pulpit Commentary on Matthew*, pages 580-581 .

16. Matthew Henry in his *Commentary on Matthew's Gospel*, page 138.

17. *The Pulpit Commentary on Mark's Gospel*, pages 119-120.

18. Rev. S. Conway in *The Pulpit Commentary on the Revelation,* pg.78.

19. *Fresh Wind-Fresh Fire,* by Joe Cymbala, published by Zondervan Publishing House, Grand Rapids, MI.

20. Rev. S. Conway in *The Pulpit Commentary on the Revelation,* pg. 78

21. Adam Clarke in his *Commentary on the Revelation*, page 981.

22. Ibid., page 915.

23. Matthew Henry in his *Commentary on the Revelation*, page 911.

24. Verses by S. Conway

25. David Wilkerson in *America's Last Call*, pages 54 and 55, published by Wilkerson Trust Publications, P.O. Box 260, Lindale, TX.

26. Ibid, page 147, pg. 2